Misty Memories

The Autobiography

Misty Rowe

England Media
Hendersonville, TN

Misty Memories – The Autobiography
by Misty Rowe with Scot England

ISBN: 978-0-9986367-6-4

Editor: Steve Jenne
Front Cover Design/ Kevin Reinhardt-BlueRhinoCreative.com
Front Cover Photo/ Joe Arce/Starstruck Foto – The Hollywood Show
Back Cover Design/Layout: Paula Underwood Winters
Back cover photo/ Misty and Cornfield courtesy Jeremy Westby
Thank you to Diane Lovullo for numerous Hee Haw photos

Printed in the United States of America

For more info on Misty Rowe, visit www.mistyrowe.com

Published by:
England Media
102 Rachels Ct
Hendersonville TN 37075

If you enjoyed this book, you will also like these autobiographies published by England Media:

Lulu Roman "This Is My Story; This Is My Song"
Jimmy Capps "The Man in Back"
Ronnie McDowell "Bringing It to You Personally"
Johnny Lee "Still Lookin' for Love"
Moe Bandy "Lucky Me"
Larry Black "The Cameras Weren't Always Rollin'"

CONTENTS

DEDICATION

I dedicate this book to my daughter Dreama. She was born after my television career in 1992...the "Year of the Woman." Dreama has always wanted to know the story of how I made it. I think that can be summed up in one word – Hope. Dreama's name means "Hope." For all the parts I have played in my lifetime, my greatest role was being her mom.

When I was a little girl, I wanted to be a writer. I also dreamed of becoming an actress.

I used to write little shows, and I put them on in our garage for the neighborhood kids. My always-creative mother, Rosie, nailed up her clothesline and put sheets over it, so I would have a stage curtain to open and close.

My childhood was often a jumble of love and violence. To escape the latter, I would create a fantasy world where dreams could come true.

I left home with $27 and a pair of cut-off jeans. What happened to my dreams…you are about to read. What happened in my real life…I am finally willing to share.

So how did you spend the great quarantine, lock down of 2020? I'm sure that many people caught up on their reading. You could have read a bunch of books during all that craziness when we were stuck inside.

But instead of reading a book…I decided to write one…my autobiography. You have it in your hands right now. Yes, you have my life in your hands.

While I was writing this book, I also celebrated a birthday. It was what they call a milestone birthday. It was a number that most actresses, and especially former sex symbols would never admit to. I turned 70. Oh my God. There it is. Right on the paper for all the world to see. Yes, Misty Rowe is 70 years old.

Over the years, as I've done personal appearances and autograph signings, many people have come up to me saying, "You need to write a book. You have had such an interesting life." I always told them I probably wasn't up to it. While I have written many plays and stage productions, I knew that writing your autobiography is a totally different deal.

As I headed for my 7th decade, it was really my daughter Dreama who pushed me to get my life story on paper. She said, "Mommy, it's really time. You need to write a book." I asked her, "Who is going to buy it?" She smiled, "I will!" Well, there's one.

There was a serious reason behind my daughter's request. She explained, "Mom, you know Alzheimer's runs in our family. Nana got it." Dreama called my mother Nana. Mom got Alzheimer's when she was 80.

As only daughters can do, Dreama continued to be her usual honest, but very blunt self, saying, "What if that happens to you? You won't be able to remember the wonderful things in your life. But if you had a book, I could read those memories back to you."

Well, hopefully that day will never come. As I write this, my memory is still very good. One of the strongest talents I've had throughout my career was my ability to memorize dialogue very quickly. I could also remember places and events from decades ago. That comes in very handy when you are writing your life story. Oddly enough, I've always had a hard time with people's names. During our Hee Haw days, my friend Marianne Gordon Rogers told me, "When you meet someone, you should go into another room and write their name down on your arm. They will think you're rude if you forget their name." Of course, if they saw their name written on your arm, they would think you were crazy!

Having said all that, I think I chose a pretty good title for this book. One great blessing in writing this came when I started going through my old memorabilia. My mother had kept every photo, newspaper and magazine clipping from my childhood and through most of my career. Before she went into a nursing home, she gave it all to me. It was an unbelievable gift.

I also had boxes and boxes of scrapbooks and photo albums that I hadn't looked at in decades. You'll see many of those photos in this book. No one has ever seen them before, except me and my parents.

Going through all those old boxes evoked a lifetime of memories. I would pick up a photo and say, "Oh my God. I remember that now. I hadn't thought about that moment for years." As I thumbed through the faded, yellowing press clippings, I knew that my daughter was right. It would be a shame if all my memories were lost forever.

I always had a dream. I always had a dream of what I wanted to be and where I wanted to go. Lots of those came true, some more than I could have ever imagined. But others did not. Life is not all roses. Of course, I spent a large part of my life in a cornfield, and you won't find many roses in a cornfield!

There are many, many other actresses and performers who have had bigger and more successful careers than I have had. But there is no one who had more fun in their career than I did. In my life and career, I made some good decisions and I also made some horrible ones. I have no regrets.

But if I was going to write my story, I wanted it to be honest. I want to be open with you. There are some things that weren't very pleasant in my life. I've had ups and downs, probably an equal amount of both. I know that everyone has hardships in their life, and I hope that my willingness to talk about my struggles might help someone else.

There is a saying that I kind of live by, that's based on a quote by Morgan Harper Nichols. It is, "One day you will tell your story of how you overcame what you went through and it can become someone else's survival guide." I guess today is the day that I tell my story.

– Love, Misty

INTRODUCTION

"As a writer, you pray for the chance to write for someone like Misty. She always delivers, and she makes what you write funnier by her interpretation. Comedy history has not produced too many beautiful people who are also funny. Lucille Ball, Cary Grant, and Marilyn Monroe are a few. I would add Misty to that select list.

Like the other icons mentioned, Misty is an actor first. She knows how to create a character and instill it with believability, and that's what makes her so successful.

I will add that, off camera, she is a delight as well: no tantrums, no diva moments, just pure professionalism. I count myself lucky to have worked with her."

– Barry Adelman / Executive Vice President,
Dick Clark Productions Television

FOREWORD

In 1972, I interviewed for a role on Hee Haw. While there, I met another actress. She said her name was Misty Rowe. I smiled and said, "I thought you said Misty Rose." I don't remember her exact words, but in a very polite way, she let me know that it was definitely not Misty Rose. I liked that because I took it as meaning she was happy that she had a name that was more substantial than one made up for Hollywood.

Fortunately, they were looking for more than one actress, so when I arrived in Nashville, Misty was also there. In my opinion, she was the quintessential Hee Haw girl: blonde, shapely, a big smile, and a voice that had laughter running through each sentence. We were there for six weeks, and at one point, Misty asked if she could borrow twenty dollars. Paying someone back was not a high priority in Hollywood, but I liked Misty so much, I was happy to loan it to her. We got to know each other well. We spent every day together, working, and ate dinner most nights with the other girls. To my surprise, when we started back to L.A., Misty paid me back the twenty dollars – plus five dollars interest!

A short time later, we all returned to tape another season. It was great to see everybody and catch up on what we had all been doing. Everyone, however, wanted to talk to Misty. She had just bought a house in the Hollywood canyons. I was so happy for her – and amazed! As I got to know her better, and became close friends with her, I visited her home in L.A. It was quite charming. A few years later, she sold that home and purchased another one in the Hollywood Hills – an even better investment. This blue-eyed blonde not only had talent, she also had a head for business!

Since then, Misty and I have remained close friends. I was part of her wedding and she was part of mine. We talk several times a year and it is always a joy. I can still hear her voice over the phone saying, "Mary-Anne?" I consider her a rare and endearing friend, and I feel incredibly honored to have been so close to her for all these years. She has a fantastic life story and I am honored to write this foreword. If even half of her charm and charisma come across in this book, as I'm sure it will, you are in for a real treat.

Marianne G. Rogers

A STAR IS BORN…IN A BARN?

"I was born in the middle of a cornfield. I was the love child of Junior Samples and Lulu Roman."

I always wanted to say that!

I wasn't really born in a cornfield. But I did live in a barn when I was a baby. My dad was from the Missouri Ozarks and Mom was from Chicago. When they first got married, they made their home out of a barn. My mom fixed it up real cute, and they lived there until I was about a year old. There was an old church mission near their home, and my older brother was the person who pulled the rope on the mission bell to call people to church.

I was born in San Gabriel, California on June 4, 1950. The small hospital where I was born had a daily newspaper and the paper headline that day read, "A Star Is Born to the Edward Rowes."

I was born Linda Marie Rowe, and while the newspaper might have thought I was a star, I was also a very sick little girl. I had a heart murmur that went unnoticed and untreated. The first sign of trouble came during my baptism. My Uncle Herbert, who was my godfather, held me in his arms during the ceremony. As soon as it concluded, he said, "This child is sick, and you have to take her to a doctor."

Thanks to my observant uncle and thanks to the fairly new drug called penicillin, I was able to recover.

It's funny the things you remember when you start writing your life story. The very earliest memory I have is of my mother singing in the kitchen, as she washed my hair. She laid me on the counter over the kitchen sink and after shampooing my hair, she would rinse it with a concoction of vinegar and warm water. It stunk something terrible! I'd cover my eyes with a towel, and she'd sing, "I'm making a salad, I'm making a salad," as she poured more vinegar over my head.

Real salads were a luxury my mother never got to make for us. My family was very poor, and never had any money. Instead of a salad, one of our most frequent meals was a small bowl of ketchup soup. Mom boiled water and then squeezed ketchup into it. Once you stirred it up real good, it was actually kind of tasty.

My mother used to tell me that Dad would give her ten dollars per child, and that was how much she had to spend on our clothes for the entire year. To make do, my mom was always on the lookout for clothes of any kind, from anywhere. Much of our clothing came from trashcans, after someone had thrown them out. Mom would find a shirt or pants, take them home and wash and iron them, and we would have a new (to us) outfit.

But my brothers and I had a plush life compared to my mom. Mother was born in 1919. She was one of nine children. My grandmother Sophie had been married to a very wealthy man, but he was a drunkard who cheated on her. When he raised his fist to her, that was it for grandma. She put all the kids on a horse and buggy and left. My grandfather came running out and grandma took a horse whip to him.

2

Grandma didn't have the money to raise so many kids, so she put some of them, including my mom in foster homes. Later, when she tried to get them back, the couple who took in my mom, refused to give her up. But grandma kept fighting for her, and she finally had to take the couple to court, where she regained custody of her daughter.

Grandmother ended up running a laundry. Since she couldn't work and take care of all of her children, she made my mom quit school. Mom had just started high school and her teacher came to the laundry and begged my grandmother to let Rosie go to school, because she was very bright. And my grandma said, "I can't. I have nine children, and Rosie has to watch five of them, so I can work to put food on the table."

But even during those very hard times of the Great Depression, my family still found joy. My Uncle Chuck, Mom's younger brother, remembers that every Saturday night, after supper, they would roll up the carpet and my grandmother would play the piano and they'd all dance in the living room. Mom loved to dance, and after she moved to California, she and her brother Johnny were in dance contests on Catalina Island.

Grandma would eventually remarry a wonderful man named Dave. He was from Sweden, and when he passed through Ellis Island in 1898, the immigration officials asked his name. When he gave his name, they couldn't pronounce or spell it. So, they asked what his dad's name was, and when he said "John," they wrote "John's son,", so grandpa's name became Dave Johnson. Grandpa Dave also fought in World War 1.

During the war, my mom worked as a riveter. She always thought she was the famous "Rosie the Riveter," but that turned out to be another Rosie.

For a time, we lived in a little house in Covina, California. My father was able to get a loan for the house since he was a war veteran. They had a veteran's bill that allowed him to purchase the home without putting any money down.

Our little home had just two bedrooms. My older brother Eddie and I slept in bunk beds in one room. But when my little brother Bob was born, there was no room for me in the bedroom. So, I grew up without a room of my own. I had to sleep on a small cot in the living room.

Since I was right next to the television, I would turn it on, with the sound down low, so no one would know I was up, and I would watch old movies, especially any with Fred Astaire and Ginger Rogers. I would watch Fred in his tuxedo and Ginger in her elegant gowns, and I'd look down at my nightgown that Mom had gotten out of a trashcan. I cried myself to sleep, and then dreamed of wearing a beautiful outfit and being in the movies.

My mom was a devout Catholic and I went to a Catholic school. I was educated by nuns for eight years. I don't know how Mom got us in that school, because we certainly didn't have the money to go there. But the Catholic church would occasionally waive the tuition for people who couldn't pay it. So, I went to the Sacred Heart School during my elementary and junior high school years, and I had to learn all my prayers in Latin.

When I was born, one of my legs was wrapped around the other, and it took them so long to get them apart, that when I started walking, I had a funny, kind of pigeon walk. Mom was so afraid that the other kids would make fun of me, that she asked a doctor if anything could be done for me. He told her that I needed to strengthen my leg muscles. He suggested that I take ballet or some form of dancing Of course, we didn't have any money for such an extravagance. But that did not stop my mother.

Back in the 1950s, people didn't have clothes dryers. They hung all their laundry outside on a clothesline and let the wind and sun dry everything. One day, Mom noticed a lot of clothes on the line of the local dance teacher. Mom knocked on her door and introduced herself, and then explained, "I've got three kids, no money and a girl with a bad leg. I used to run a laundry in Chicago, and I can iron clothes better than anyone I know." Then she offered, "I will iron all of your family's clothes in exchange for ballet lessons for my daughter."

Years later, when someone would compliment me with, "You have the most beautiful legs in the world," I would always think back to everything my mother did to make sure I could walk like a normal child. Willie Billmeyer took my mom up on her offer, and from that moment on, Willie became a wonderful part of my life. She started giving me two ballet lessons each week. Then she gave me tap dance lessons, followed by jazz dancing.

Willie's family was very well-to-do, and she had a daughter named Cathy, who was very popular. Cathy was four years older than I, and when she outgrew her clothes, Willie would bring them over for me. I was so happy to have pretty clothes for the first time. I didn't even mind that they were just a little big for me. I knew I would eventually grow into them.

All these years later, I still remember Willie's kindness to me, especially on Christmas Eve. Our family didn't have money for any gifts…none. But Willie's brother ran a toy store, and after he closed on Christmas Eve, Willie went to his store and bought all the toys that hadn't sold. Then she brought them all to our house. She was ringing bells and shouting "Ho! Ho! Ho!" Because of Willie, Christmas Eve is still my favorite day of the entire year.

Willie did so many things for me. She sewed all the costumes I needed for all of my dance recitals, when she knew our family couldn't afford to pay her. She took me to an ice-skating show, and when I was 8 years old, she took me to see the musical movie "Gigi." As I looked up at the giant screen, I was in awe of Leslie

Caron's beauty. Ten years later, I would get to meet Leslie in person, but you'll have to wait until the next chapter to read about that encounter.

My brother Eddie was three years older than I, and my brother Bobby was five years younger. When my parents wanted to go out for the evening, they couldn't afford a babysitter, but they thought Eddie was old enough to watch us. Before Mom and Dad left, Mom said we could each have the rare treat of a Hostess Twinkie.

But the moment my parents pulled out of the driveway, Eddie grabbed Bobby and stuffed him in our laundry hamper. He slid it under the sink, so Bobby couldn't lift the lid. Then Eddie grabbed me and threw me in the closet. He tied his belt around the door handle, so I was stuck inside. As Bobby and I screamed, Eddie sat down at the kitchen table and ate all three of our Twinkies. My brother remembers this to this day.

As we got older, my parents wanted to go out once a week and go dancing. My father instructed Eddie, "You are in charge. Don't let those kids leave the house until we get back." I guess Eddie did as Dad told him, but his method left much to be desired. He went up on the roof, with his B.B. gun, and when Bobby and I ran out to play in the yard, Eddie shot us both!

When Eddie was 18, he joined the Air Force. I'm sure his B-B-gun shooting skills helped him when he went into the Air Corps. He now lives in South Carolina, while Bobby calls Lake Havasu, Arizona home.

Mom gave me the nickname of Misty when I was a little girl, because I cried all the time. I continued using Misty when I became best friends with a girl named Linda. Since we both had the same first name, I told her to call me Misty. As we exchanged pen pal letters during our teen years, I signed each one as Misty.

My father was short, but a handsome man. He looked like Steve McQueen, with blue eyes and natural blonde hair. I inherited my blonde hair from him. Most of the Rowes are from Missouri, and Daddy was born in Marionville, Missouri. His mother was part Cherokee and was raised on a reservation. She died after drinking bad water from a well. She died from diphtheria when my father was just a year and a half old. With no mother, and his father having to work, Dad was sent to live with his uncle. I always felt sorry for my dad, because I know he had a very strange and sad childhood.

Dad did his best to provide for us, but he had one problem. He drank alcohol. His drinking usually ended with a shouting (or worse) match with my mother. Since I slept in the living room, I unfortunately had a front-row seat for some violent incidents. I'd wake up in the middle of the night to my mom screaming as Dad beat her. My brother Eddie would run in and try to pull dad away from Mom. Dad then turned his attention to Eddie, and he beat up my brother pretty bad.

The next morning, all was quiet in our home, and no one dared mention what had taken place hours before. We also told no one outside our home. But people knew. Our neighbors had two kids, but they weren't allowed to play with us, because their parents had heard my parents fighting.

I loved my father so much. I looked just like him and I was a Missouri towhead, like my daddy. Dad could be so sweet and wonderful, but when he drank, he could go into a rage that would scare us all. Most of his violence was directed toward mom and Eddie. He would hit Eddie with his fist, and I saw him throw my mother across the entire room.

When Mom was pregnant with my younger brother, she found out Dad was fooling around with another woman. I was too young to know what was happening, and one day, as I saw Dad getting ready to leave for his next rendezvous, I secretly went out and got into the backseat of his car. I laid on the floor as he drove for about ten minutes, then I happily jumped up and yelled, "Hi Daddy!" When he got to his girlfriend's home, he actually took me inside and made me sleep with her kids!

The next morning, he dropped me off at home on his way to work. When I walked in, my worried-sick mother asked, "Misty, where have you been all night?" I truthfully answered, "With Daddy, at a nice lady's house."

When my father returned home, my parents had a fight like never before. Dad demanded that we all get in the car, and he drove us up to Mt. Baldy Mountain. The farther he drove, the angrier he got. He told Mom he was going to drive us all over a cliff. Mom grabbed the steering wheel and they fought back and forth as our car repeatedly swerved across the centerline and from one ditch to the other.

Dad stopped the car and started strangling Mom. Eddie was trying to pry Dad's hands from her neck. I stood up on the backseat floor and made my hands into little fists. I reached over the front seat and pounded my dad's back, screaming, "Stop, Daddy stop!" It was a terrifying incident that finally ended when Dad came to his senses. In addition to his drinking, I'm sure that he was also bi-polar, but that was a term none of us had heard back then.

In addition to ironing clothes for the neighbors, my mother made a little money scrubbing floors and watering people's lawns. She would use that money to give my brothers and me a quarter allowance each week. We usually spent that 25 cents at the local movie theater. My brothers loved cowboys, so almost every movie we watched was a Western. When we pooled our money, we had enough for just one box of candy, and each week, my older brother instructed, "Nobody gets any candy until someone gets shot."

When I was nine years old, as we settled in to watch the latest cowboy film, the trailers for upcoming movies began to roll. I stared as a 12-foot-high bosomy blonde started singing. I looked at each of my brothers and their eyes were as big as saucers. The movie was "Some Like It Hot" and the blonde was of course, Marilyn Monroe.

When that film came out, our Catholic church condemned it, meaning it was so tawdry and sexually explicit that we would lose our souls if we watched it. So, of course, I wanted to see it! I thought Marilyn was so cute, funny and adorable. I had no idea what an important part of my life she would later become.

My Grandpa came to visit us, and as soon as he walked in, he couldn't believe that I, now ten, was sleeping on a cot in the middle of the living room. He announced, "She is a young lady, who needs her own room, and I'm going to build it." Grandpa expanded and sealed in our front porch, and that tiny space, less than 10 feet across, became my room. My cot took up the entire room, and I had to put all my clothes in the coat closet in the hallway. Besides the small size, there was an even bigger problem. When visitors stepped inside our front door, they were actually walking right into my bedroom! Every time someone rang the doorbell, I had to get out of bed and open the door, so they could come in….to my room. It was a pretty crazy setup, but at least I had my own little space.

One of my most traumatic moments of childhood came when I was nine years old. And before it was all over, my dad would make the situation much, much worse.

We were visiting my Grandpa and Grandma in Covina and had planned to have Sunday dinner after church. There was a park in between the church and Grandma Sophie's. I told mom that I was going to make the short walk through the park by myself while she went to the market to pick up a couple things for our meal.

At the time, I had long blonde hair, down my back. Everyone always commented on how pretty my hair was. As I was walking through the park, a man ran up and covered my mouth with one hand, while he tried to touch me in an inappropriate way. He sneered, "If you scream, I'll cut you." But the moment he dropped his hand, I screamed as loud as I could. He ran one way and I ran straight to Grandma's.

Instead of calling the police, my father said, "It's her hair. It is attracting people that shouldn't be attracted to her. She's too young for that long hair." The next day, he dragged a kitchen chair out into the backyard. He put a bath towel around my shoulders and started to cut my hair…with a pair of gardening shears. To make my new-do even worse, he took one of mom's mixing bowls, put it on my head and cut all the hair that was sticking out under the bowl.

I cried as I watched my long, blonde curls fall to the ground. When my barber-father was done, I had quite the bowl haircut. To say the least, it did not help my popularity when I returned to school.

Through lots of hard work, my dad got a used car lot that he opened with the catchy name of "Ed Rowe's Used Cars." He also worked as a flagman at Go-Kart of America. My father built his own go-carts and ran them on alcohol, instead of gas. His vehicles were always the fastest ones on the track. It was through his job that I met my first celebrity.

While Dad supervised everyone as they raced their go-carts, my mom did the cooking for the facility's snack bar. When I was ten years old, mom asked me to be the counter girl and take orders from customers. As I was serving hot dogs and Cokes, I heard a bunch of girls screaming. I asked what was going on and a man said, "Oh, Paul Newman is here. He wants to learn how to race a go-cart."

He drove in my father's go-cart, and then he came inside the snack bar and ordered a sloppy-joe and a drink. He paid for it and he left a dime on the counter as he said, "Honey, that's for you." I saved that dime for a long time, until I needed it to buy something. Of course, Paul Newman would go on to have a very successful racing career, in addition to being one of the great actors of our time.

Like many kids, I enjoyed going to the movies a lot more than I liked going to school. I wasn't a good student. In addition to my leg, I had a very high voice and a terrible lisp. I had trouble with my smile and had to wear a retainer, but even that didn't cure the big space in between my two front teeth. I was quite a mess, and it all combined to make me very self-conscious. I didn't want to talk in front of people, and when I was 13, I was asked to do much more than that.

We moved to Glendora, California, where I was put in a public school for the first time. The nuns who had always taught me, were replaced by teachers wearing short skirts. But the most frightening change came during gym class. After our hour of exercises, we were instructed to "hit the showers." To make things even more embarrassing, the P.E. teacher lined all of us up after our shower, to "make sure we had gotten wet enough."

I was horrified. I didn't know any of these girls. I hadn't grown up with them, and I didn't want them to see me naked. In an effort to get out of P.E. class, I simply cut school. After skipping classes for a week, the school, quite ironically, suspended me.

When I returned to school, a counselor met with me and asked what I might be interested in doing in school. I told them I would like to be in the drama class. It was a decision that totally changed my life. The drama teacher was Harriet Reiner. Over the next three years, Mrs. Reiner became like my second mother.

Mrs. Reiner taught me play production, children's theater, and she made me a director. I ran the drama club snack bar and I painted the scenery. And I got the lead in almost every school play we did.

At the end of my Junior year, we had to take part in a speech contest, and I was terrified. For a shy girl, with a high, squeaky voice and a lisp, it was a nightmare. But Mrs. Reiner came up with the idea to enter me in the "Humorous Interpretation" speech category. I did a monologue from the children's book "Eloise," and I took first place. Then I went to the Regional contest and I won the top spot. Finally, I competed in State, and I won that. I couldn't believe it. That came with a $100 scholarship to San Fernando Valley State. I went there for their summer session.

As my confidence grew, I asked my mother if I could attend a modeling school. She thought that was a great idea, even though it was quite pricey. I promised her that I would pay back all the money when I got my first real job. In order to pay the bill, Mom took a job working in a factory. She spent the day gluing resin grapes together for artificial fruit and flower displays.

She soon found out that the resin she worked with gave her a terrible headache. When she came home each day, she'd have to lie on the couch. All of mom's friends told her she was foolish, putting in such long hours, when there was no way I would ever pay her back.

My mom couldn't have done anymore for me. But Dad was still dealing with his drinking issues. With my brother gone to the Air Force, some of Dad's drunken, violent outbursts now headed my way. When I was 16, he got angry and hit me in the chest with his fist. When he raised back to hit me a second time, I ran screaming, out of the house.

I had no place to run to, but I decided that I was not going to go back home, where I would probably be beaten. I found a vacant garage and stayed there for three days and nights. I finally called my mom and she convinced me to come back. I guess you could say that our family was not like the Ingalls on Little House on the Prairie.

Before I move on to some of my more exciting teen years, I have one more story about my mother.

In 1933, my mom's brother Johnny took her to the Chicago World's Fair. During their day at the fair, they sneaked in to see the famous burlesque dancer Sally Rand.

Fifty years later, when we were living in Glendora, California, Mom went to a garage sale, searching for some clothes for me. While she was there, Mom found a playbill of Sally Rand. She picked it up and went up to the old woman who was running the sale. Mom shared the story of seeing Sally Rand at the World's Fair. She also explained, "That's why I'm paying for dance lessons for my daughter. I will never forget how beautiful Sally was."

When Mom asked how much she wanted for the playbill, the old woman said, "There's no charge. I liked your story." Then she stunned Mother when she asked, "Would you like me to sign it to your daughter? I'm Sally Rand." I still have that program today, and I still smile when I read, "To Misty, Sally Rand".

I would eventually turn that playbill and my mother's story into a stage production, and I'll tell you about that later in this book.

My mother holds Linda Marie Rowe. You can call me Misty.

My first swimming pool.

Trying to figure things out at one year old.

Already an animal lover, at age 2.

Feeding turkeys at 2 years old.

My father plays with me and Eddie.

A happy photo session with my brother Eddie.

My brother
Eddie was 5. I
was 3 years old.

A rare photo of me
with both my broth-
ers, Eddie and Bob.

No wonder I felt comfortable in the Hee Haw Kornfield! I'm on the front right, 1955.

Eddie and I pretend we are space aliens. I'm the alien on the right.

My dad cut my hair for these school photos. He always made sure to get the bangs perfectly straight!

Alice in Wonderland, senior year. I'm on the front right.

With my champion, Mrs. Reiner.

The photo I sent to KBLA to audition for the Teenage Fair.

High school play
The Diary of
Adam and Eve.

I would use material from this dress to make a sarong for my bikini.

"LOVE MAKES THE WORLD GO 'ROUND" 1968

High school sweetheart Dennis Cardwell, heading to Vietnam.

My first
Sal-ute!
Wearing
Dennis' Marine
hat.

Appearing in my
first professional
play.

Contestant #24 in the Miss Wahini Bikini pageant.

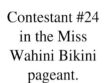

Wearing the sarong I made from my prom dress, Oct. 1968. Photo by Marvin Hayden.

Modeling one of
my pageant
prizes.

Riding in the Santa
Claus Lane parade in
Hollywood.

Posing next to Charlie
See, who helped me see
the world.

Posing with my Miss Wahini Bikini trophy and Laugh-In's Gary Owens.

Arriving in my cowgirl outfit at the Moomba Festival in Melbourne, Australia.

Making friends with Miss Hawaii.

Teaching the Australian Lord Mayor to go-go dance.

Jumping for joy. Photo by Charlie See.

This photo of me leap-frogging over Miss Mexico ran in newspapers around the world.

Showing off a few of my beauty queen trophies.

One of my professional photo shoots.

Photo by Peter Gowland

Playing piano for our can-can group. Photo by Leonard Ashmore.

Promoting the Lens
Clickers Club,
1968

Girl Next Door

A salty photo for the
cover of Overdrive
trucker's magazine.

Miss Rigid Tool!

With my parrot I named Bogart. Ironically, a few years later, I would be in a movie that had Bogart in the title.

In the play Take Her, She's Mine.

Getting top billing at the Hollywood Theater

Publicity photo for The Hitchhikers, 1972

Magazine ads for the PK Ski Company.

Photo by Peter Gowland

Introducing the New Red, Red Baron

Magazine ads for the PK Ski Company.

Photo by Peter Gowland

Outside the 44th Academy Awards with Robert Amram.

A polaroid photo of my first day on the Hee Haw set.

My very first time in the Kornfield.

My first official Hee Haw photo.

In the Kornfield with Hugh Hefner.

On a lunch break with Barbie Benton.

On my way to another audition, July 1972.

Photo session I did before my audition for Goodbye, Norma Jean. Photo by Buddy Rosenberg

On the cover of the Australasian Post magazine.

Publicity shot as the young Marilyn in Goodbye, Norma Jean.

A day of modeling can wear a girl out.

Recreating Marilyn's famous subway dress photo.

Photo by Suze Randall

With James
DePaiva. We were
the perfect couple...
until we weren't.

Introducing James to
Elton John.

Wedding day. (L-R) Birgita, my gown designer, high school friend Cyndee Milligan, Misty, Drama teacher Harriet Reiner, Dance teacher Willie Billmeye

My bridesmaids. Mary Jo Thatcher, Barbie Benton, Cathy Billmeyer, Marianne Rogers, Misty, Peggy Rochelle.

Marianne Rogers and her son Christopher, Misty, Barbie Benton and my flower girl Marlo Milligan.

The bride and groom.

The great Kenny Rogers took this portrait of me as a wedding gift.

Whether I am directing or acting, you will always find me smiling!

Robin Leach invited my husband and I to appear on his LIfestyles of the Rich and Famous show.

A behind the scenes photo showing our cue card guy Martin Clayton and Jackie Phelps and Charley Pride.

Our Fit as a Fiddle sketch with Irlene Mandrell and Gunilla Hutton.

Working out with the King of Country Music, Roy Acuff.

Sam Lovullo. Through our ups and downs, he was always my Papa Sam.

Misty's Bedtime
Stories. My
co-author, Scot
England now owns
the bed.

Roy Clark and
Roy Acuff lead
sing-a-long.

Kenny Rogers and
Hee Haw Honeys
Barbie Benton,
Marianne Gordon
Rogers, Linda
Thompson, Misty
Rowe.

My husband surprises me as he dresses up as a gorrila.

Charlie Chase filmed the prank for his Funny Business show.

This is one of the last photos of Junior Samples on the Hee Haw set. It was taken in June of 1983, and Junior passed away that November.

Photo courtesy of Danny Forbes.

Regis Philbin, Kathy Lee Gifford and Roy Clark. Regis passed away as I was writing this book.

With Sid Caesar
at his Dinner
Theatre.

Vicki Lawrence
hosts a birthday
party for me.

My equity agent, and true friend, Joan Kovats. I love Joan so much.

With football legend Joe Namath in Li'l Abner.

Starring as Daisy Mae with Joe Namath in Li'l Abner.
Photos by Paul Buckholdt.

In a promotional
shot with Tom
Neilson for Pump
Boys and
Dinettes.

Musical Director
ck Bourgault leads
he curtain call for
the Michigan
oduction of Pump
Boys and Dinettes

I loved portraying waitress Rhetta Cup and working with Coralee Troutwine.

Playing John Houseman's love interest in Silver Spoons.
Photo Courtesy NBC-TV

"Misty is, in sum, Star material."

Dallas Times Herald

"Lola is played by Misty Rowe who is so sensational-looking it makes you appreciate, for once, the view a theatre-in-the-round affords."

Jeremy Gerard
The Dallas Morning News

"... 'Damn Yankees.' It's a big friendly American hot dog of a show ... It's got solid performers up and down the lineup, including Misty Rowe, the sizzling little lambchop of "Hee Haw" fame. One example will capsulize how nothing seems capable of going wrong in this production in 'Whatever Lola Wants,' Miss Rowe takes one of her frilly garments and tosses it backward between her legs, so that it sails over Joe's shoulder and makes a perfect three-point landing on a wall hook. **Not since Astaire made his cane fly across the room into an umbrella stand has there been a neater toss.** So: predict Miss Rowe will be offered two sports contracts, one from the Cowboys, who could use a back-up center, and one from the Rangers, who could use a control pitcher."

Dan Hulbert,
Dallas Times Herald

"What a wonderful Lola you've come up with! I hope we can do something in the future soon again — I would find it a joy! Meanwhile, include me in as a fan most ardent with admiration and respect and love."
Buff Shurr
Director of "Damn Yankees"
Granny's Dinner Playhouse

Thank You
Joan Kosrato!

Equity:
Exclusive Artists Agency

Theatrical:
Charter Management

Full page ad in Variety promoting me in Damn Yankees.

With Dallas Cowboy Harvey Martin in Damn Yankees.

One of my favorite skits with Lulu Roman and Williams & Ree.

Working with
7-foot, 2-inch
Richard Kiel in
Taipei.

Kenny Rogers was a wonderful photographer. He took this photo
and then gave it to me.

Another portrait by Kenny Rogers.

With my fan club president Julius Kovats and Johnny
Crawford from The Rifleman.

Introducing my fan club president, Julius Kovats, to Loretta Lynn.

With Christopher Knight in Joe's World.

With Jan-Michael Vincent on Airwolf.

A four handed operator in the TV series Quark.

Misty at 47 years old.

Photo by Marc Raboy

One of my favorite photos.

Photo by Marc Raboy

Christmas Eve with my Aunt Gertie and Mama Rosie.

3 great friends. Didi Reuben, Misty, Barbie Benton.

Wearing my infamous red dress for a photo shoot by Kenny Rogers.

My pride and joy. My 1936 Cord Roadster.

The amazing Stella Adler. The woman who taught me so much about acting and about life.

I was so happy that Stella Adler got to meet my daughter.

I will always treasure this photo of Stella holding my baby.

Lions and
Tigers and,
my daughte
Dreama.

Going all out as I read to Dreama's class.

read to Glenville Elementary students and then they had a surprise brithday party for me.

Mom

My mom has shiney blond hair. Her eyes are green like a flield of grass. She is sweeter than a flower. She looks like a butterfly when she opens her arms to greet me. Her hair is like golden silk. Her voice is like the sound of a humming birds wings as it flies throgh the air. I love my mom.

A poem I treasure that my daughter Dreama wrote.

My brother Ed and sister-in-law Wanda with my daughter Dreama

Celebrating a birthday with Dreama.

TEEN YEARS

I'd like to tell you a little bit about my underwear.

How's that for an attention grabber?!

I met my best friend in high school drama class. Her name was Mary Jo Thatcher.

Mary Jo had also gone to a Catholic school, and now that we were growing up, we found that we shared some of the same teenage girl dreams. We both dreamed of getting out of Glendora. We wanted to leave our small town and see the world.

We also wanted to become glamorous and scandalous…even though neither one of us really knew the definition of scandalous. But we figured that if we were going to be scandalous, we would first have to learn how to be sexy.

Neither of us had a clue of how to be sexy.

But we somehow determined that our white Catholic girls school underwear was not sexy. But it could be…if it were black. We thought that black underwear would be downright scandalous!

I guess what I am about to tell you next, should come with the disclaimer of "Do not try this at home." Or anywhere else.

Mary Jo's mom worked during the day, so I went over to her house after school and we got out her mother's best roasting pan. We had skipped lunch that day so we could use our lunch money to buy a box of black hair dye. We boiled a pan of water and then dumped the dye in.

As the boiling water turned black, we added six pairs of our white underwear. In just a few minutes, our panties were cooked scandalously black. Mary Jo quickly rinsed the roasting pan and put it back in the cupboard. I got permission to stay at Mary Jo's, (so we could keep a close eye on our drying underwear in her bedroom.)

When Mary Jo's mother came home from work, she began cooking supper. As luck would have it, Mary Jo's dad was bringing his boss home, in hopes of landing a new promotion. When we came out of Mary Jo's room, we saw her mom was cooking a chicken in the roasting pan we had just used.

A half hour later, we heard a scream. Mary Jo's mother was horrified as she held up a dark blue chicken. We had not scrubbed out all the black dye from the pan, and it had seeped into the now foul fowl.

I will never forget the site of the woman standing there, holding that blue bird. She shouted at me and Mary Jo, "Girls, this is scandalous!" I guess, at least now, we knew what the word meant.

The next time you see me, please let me know if you can ever eat chicken again without thinking of Misty Rowe's underwear!

In 1965, my parents gave me permission to go out on my first car date. It was a big moment for a 15-year-old girl. The boy who asked me out was named Bobby Maloney. I wanted to look my best for Bobby, so I put on lip gloss and my first pair of high heeled shoes. I was so excited…until Bobby stopped for gas.

As he got out of the car to head to the fuel pump, Bobby casually said, "You are cute. But you're not as pretty as my last girlfriend." As he pumped his gas, I sat in the passenger seat, completely devastated...in my new high heels.

As I tried to keep from crying, I turned on the car radio. At that moment, I heard a commercial that shouted, "You can be a go-go dancer for the world-famous Teenage Fair at the Hollywood Palladium! Send your picture, name and phone number into KBLA, in care of Teen Beat magazine."

Bobby got back in the car, and we went on our first date. The entire time, all I could think about was getting back home, so I could send my info into that contest. I'm sure that many girls submitted glossy 8 x 10 photos, but I had nothing like that. Since we never had a lot of money for pictures, the best I could come up with was my 8th grade graduation, Catholic school photo. To make it even worse, it was the size of a postage stamp! But I glued that tiny black and white photo to a plain postcard, and hand wrote my name and phone number on it.

I sent that postcard off to Teen Beat magazine, and a couple weeks later, KBLA called to tell me I had "won the chance to audition for the Teenage Fair." My mother drove me to Sunset and Vine in Hollywood, where we saw the other 2, 000 "contest winners" who had been invited to try out.

They divided the teenage girls into 100 groups of 20. Then they started playing music and the girls danced. After a minute, they cut 5 girls and then started the music again. Then they cut some more girls and instructed the remaining ones to continue dancing. At the end of the day, I was one of the very last girls still standing (and dancing).

A man came up and announced, "Young lady, you will be dancing at the Palladium! Do you have a Social Security number?" I answered, "No, but I can get one. What is it?"

The Hollywood Palladium had an art deco stage, with an 11, 000 square foot dance floor. Since I was hired to be a go-go dancer, I went to Sears and bought a cheap pair of plastic boots that went up to my knees. I also wore my favorite mini-skirt.

When I arrived at the Teenage Fair, I was surprised to learn that I would be dancing in a tower, 50 feet above the stage. I was even more surprised when I learned that I would be dancing as some very big-name acts performed live. During the next week, I danced behind groups including The Bee Gees, Sonny and Cher, and The Young Rascals.

One night, as I was dancing high up in the air, I heard someone yelling my name from the ground. I looked down and it was my first car date, Bobby Maloney. I just kept dancing.

My mother was so proud that all the dance lessons she had paid for were now paying off. The Teenage Fair organizers were so impressed with me, that the next year, they invited me back to be in their fashion show as a runway model.

But my next taste of fame was not as pleasant.

I heard that a motion picture was looking for extras and if you were chosen, not only would you be in the movie, but you would also get a free lunch. The movie starred Leslie Caron, whom I had loved in "Gigi" when I was a little girl.

The extras were needed for a party scene, so I put on the very best dress I owned. When I got to the shooting location, the director escorted Leslie Caron through the crowd of extras. As she passed by, she pointed at me and my best dress, and she said, "Put her in the back." I was heartbroken. Not many people saw me in that movie. But I did get the free lunch.

One of my dearest, life-long friends was a girl named Linda Gibson, from Frankfort, Indiana. We were the same age and had the same first name of Linda. Our fathers were close friends, and one winter, during a snowstorm, Linda's dad went down to their basement to check on their water pipes that were frozen. He tried to thaw them by using a blowtorch, but it ended up burning their house down. So, even though we had only a two-bedroom home, my father invited Linda's entire family to come live with us. We put tents out in the backyard. This was back when I was having to sleep in the living room, so Linda put a sleeping bag next to my little cot.

Since we both had the same first name, to avoid confusion around our house, I started going by "Misty." When Linda's family moved back to Indiana, we wrote back and forth every week, and for my 16th birthday, I traveled to Frankfort to visit with her. A couple years later, as I was about to start my modeling and movie career, after my father had given me a speech about "not doing anything to embarrass our family name," I had my name legally changed to Misty Lin Marie Rowe.

I still stay in close touch with my friend Linda. She comes to see me anytime I perform within a state or two of her. She even sold my photos and merchandise at an event I was at a couple years ago. She is the same wonderful person she has always been, and I will treasure her friendship until the day I die.

While most students spend their time on math, history, biology and chemistry, I devoted almost all my last three high school years to plays, speech contests and stage productions. My drama teacher, and biggest supporter, Mrs. Reiner made sure to keep me busy.

My senior year, I got the lead role in "Take Her, She's Mine." I also had the lead in "Alice In Wonderland." But when it came time for them to put on "Cinderella," Mrs. Reiner came to me and explained, "Misty, of course, you would be the perfect Cinderella. But if I give you the starring role again, I will have mutiny on my hands from the other seniors and their parents." Mrs. Reiner asked if there was anything else I would like to do, and I told her, I would like to direct the play.

While I excelled with straight A's in the drama department, my grades in other subjects were just the opposite. I was doing so bad in American History, that it looked like I wasn't going to graduate. When it looked like there was no way I was going to pass the class, my teacher, Mr. Griffith told the class that for the next semester, we all had to do a special project on our own. It was up to us to come up with a thesis paper, a slide show or anything else, as long as it had to do with History.

I read through our History book and found a paragraph about Helen Hunt Jackson. Helen had written a book called "Century of Dishonor," which was about the injustices that had been done to the American Indians.

Since my grandmother had been part Cherokee, I was touched by her story and I turned it into a play. For my History project, I used our entire drama department. We made costumes and sets with pioneer cabins. Art Peterson, a classmate, helped me write it. When my history teacher saw my play, he was so impressed that he called in the principal, and then they had us put it on for the Parent-Teacher Association. The local newspaper even came out to do a feature story on it, and when I got my History grade, it had gone from an F to a B plus.

At my 20th year high school reunion, Mr. Griffith walked up to me and said, "Misty, when I start a new school year, I always tell the students about a kid who was failing, but when she applied herself, she turned everything around, and she went on to make something of her life. I am so proud of you."

My brothers Ed and Bob would also have successful careers. After leaving a sometimes-violent childhood behind, they became contractors and built good lives for their children.

Ed's daughter Teresa is not only my Godchild, but a teacher. His son Patrick is an essential worker and drives a truck for deliveries during the pandemic. This year, they finally started calling truck drivers "Heroes." But they have always been heroes to me.

My younger brother Bob's daughter Krystle worked at Hooters to put herself through graduate school. She now has a Ph.D. and is referred to as Dr. Rowe. Krystle's brother, my nephew Gary, works in construction. They all applied themselves to help others, and I am so proud of my family.

Earlier, I talked about my tap dance teacher Willie Billmeyer, who helped me in so many ways. Willie was also there for me in high school when I needed a prom dress. She hand-made me the most beautiful chiffon gown. When she was finished, she had an extra piece of chiffon material left, so she folded it up and gave it to me to keep.

My high school sweetheart Dennis Cardwell took me to the prom. Dennis was a great Christian young man. As soon as he graduated, Dennis joined the Marines. I wrote him a letter every single week that he was in Vietnam. I wrote a letter a week for almost a year and a half. We never married, but we stayed in touch over the years, and we are still close friends today.

During my senior year, Mrs. Reiner entered me in a one-act play festival at the Pasadena Playhouse. We put on a play called "The Diary of Adam and Eve" by Mark Twain. We had just three people in the entire play, and of course, I played Eve, and I covered a bikini with fig and apple leaves.

We didn't win first place at the festival. We were beat out by a group from Hollywood High, who brought in a 40-member cast (most of them playing fiddles) to put on a magnificent one-act version of "Fiddler on the Roof."

Even though we didn't take the top spot, the Pasadena Playhouse was impressed with my performance...enough to offer me a small scholarship to attend the summer semester there. I just wasn't the kind of kid who was going to go to college, and that scholarship meant everything to me.

I planned to move out of the house as soon as I graduated. My father's temper seemed to get worse every day, and I just didn't feel safe there. I planned to get a little apartment with Mary Jo while I spent the summer at the Pasadena Playhouse. But the day before I moved, I got a telegram from the Playhouse, saying they had closed. They had gone bankrupt.

I cried and cried and cried. But my father showed me no sympathy. He angrily yelled, "No more messing around! Go to work at Foster Freeze, work there and start paying rent to live here." I continued crying, thinking all of my dreams were over. At that moment, our doorbell rang.

It was my drama teacher Mrs. Reiner. She said, "Misty, come out to my car. I have something for you."

She opened her trunk and said, "I am retiring as a drama teacher. I'm going to teach English now." Mrs. Reiner told me, "Every teacher waits for that one student to come into their life, to walk in their classroom door…that one special student who they can guide and mold, and all your effort and work will mean something, because that student is the once in a lifetime student….and for me, you have been that person."

I cried as I looked into the trunk of her car, at hundreds of plays and scripts. Mrs. Reiner hugged me, saying, "This is my lifetime collection of plays. They belong to you now."

By the way, I have been carting all of those plays and scripts around, through move after move, over the past 50 years. I still have every one.

But Mrs. Reiner had one more gift for me. She whispered, "I'm so sorry about Pasadena Playhouse, but I am going to match the scholarship money that you lost. I'm going to pay to send you somewhere else."

Mrs. Reiner's husband was the cousin of the great Carl Reiner. Carl was the TV legend who was best known for creating "The Dick Van Dyke Show." Mrs. Reiner asked him where I should study and he answered, "There's only one person I would recommend. It's Estelle Harman at the Actor's Workshop."

Harriet Reiner was the person who totally changed my life. I will never forget her. I also never told her the story I'm about to tell.

Remember when this chapter started with my friend Mary Jo and me cooking our panties? Well, I thought I should end the chapter with one more scandalous stunt that Mary Jo and I had up our sleeves.

When we were in our late teens, we thought we would apply for one of our "dream jobs." I guess things like this happen after you spend eight years being raised (and disciplined) by nuns. We decided we wanted to work for the Playboy Club as drink servers...all because we wanted to wear the Playboy bunny outfit.

Of course, we knew you had to be 21 years old, and we weren't even close. I didn't even have a driver's license. So, we took our birth certificates, erased the year off our birth date and filled it in with an earlier year.

We made an appointment, and Mary Jo drove us to Playboy Enterprises in the Black Tower on Sunset Boulevard. As soon as we walked into Marilyn Grabowski's office, she asked, "How old are you girls?" We smiled and lied, "21." Marilyn exclaimed, "Ha! I cannot put you in a Playboy Club. I don't think you're of age." But before she asked us to leave, she pointed at me and said, "If you are 18, you could pose for Playboy."

I politely declined, saying, "Thank you, but I can't. I'm going to be an actress." Marilyn's smile told me she had heard that before. As Mary Jo drove us home, I had a feeling that I would see Marilyn Grabowski again.

ESTELLE AND STELLA

I was humbled by Mrs. Reiner's generosity and total faith in me as she paid for me to attend Estelle Harman's Acting Workshop.

Estelle Harman had been a casting director at Universal Studios for a dozen years, and then she opened her own acting studio. The first time I met her, I thought, 'What have I gotten myself into?' Her first question to me was, "So you want to be an actress? Do you want to do TV, film or stage?" I cheerfully chirped, "All of it! I want to do it all."

I quickly found out that Estelle told it like it was. She didn't beat around the bush and she got right to the point. "Your voice is much too high, and you will need to get rid of your lisp."

Before I could say another word, she continued, "I'm telling you right now, that you will either make it real big or you won't make it at all." I asked, "Couldn't I have something in the middle?"

"No," she said, "You are too pretty, and you're either going to be the star of the film or nobody is going to want you around, because no leading lady will want you next to her. Leading ladies don't want to be upstaged by someone who is more beautiful."

Estelle Harmon was the first person who ever told me I was beautiful. No one else ever had.

Thanks to all my work with Mrs. Reiner in high school, and now with Estelle Harman, I became very comfortable learning dialogue. I could memorize long pieces quite easily. You could give me a script and after looking it over for five minutes, I could perform it on the spot. I had an ability to memorize lines very quickly, and instead of looking down to try to find a line in the script, I could look right at the producer, director or actor I was doing a scene with. That talent helped put me ahead of many actresses I would have to audition against.

The Actor's Workshop was great because for half of the class, we did scenes from plays, and for the other half, they would put us on film. I learned about camera angles and lighting. We would also videotape our scenes and at the end of the class, Estelle would announce whom she would cast in each scene. The first time I saw myself on film and heard my voice, I wanted to crawl under the chair! I was so embarrassed when I listened to that high pitched, squeaky voice.

What would you be willing to do to pursue your dream? One of my fellow actors at Estelle Harmon was willing to live in a broom closet. Bleu McKenzie didn't have the money to enroll in the Actor's Workshop, but Estelle said he could attend if he would work as a janitor there. He agreed, but Bleu didn't have a place to live, so he stayed in the studio broom closet!

Since the Acting Workshop was located in Los Angeles, an hour away from my family home, I hoped to find a place that would be closer to my classes. Hopefully, I wouldn't end up in a closet! Once again, my high school speech and drama teacher, Mrs. Reiner, was there for me.

Mrs. Reiner said I should stay at the Hollywood Studio Club. That place had been founded by the wife of film producer David Selznick. It was basically a dormitory for young women between the ages of 17 and 25 who wanted to be actresses, singers or dancers. And it was a place for them to live safely, without being preyed upon, while they studied their craft and tried to make it in the business.

So, I paid $25 a week for a room with another girl. That price also included a daily breakfast and dinner. That seems like quite a bargain, but I was so poor that I even had trouble coming up with that small amount. When I first checked in, I had a total of $27.00, and they wanted two weeks paid in advance before you could move in.

As I started to try asking them to let me pay for only one week, I was shocked to learn that an anonymous donor had paid for my first two weeks rent. I never did find out who paid it. I thought it might have been Mrs. Reiner, but I will never know. I was also intrigued when I found out that Marilyn Monroe had once lived in the room two doors down from mine. I hoped that was a good sign!

Estelle Harman had a motto written on the arch that led into her theater. I would read that saying every day as I walked into class. It read, "The only actors who are never bad are the ones that are mediocre." That meant if you don't take chances, you will never grow. I decided right then that I was going to grow and grow, because I planned to take chances for the rest of my life.

The next year, I would meet the woman who helped me grow and who would also change my career. Her name was Stella.

Stella Adler was an amazing actress who became an even more amazing acting teacher. If you think of any of the all-time greatest actors or actresses, there's a good chance that Stella Adler taught them. Just a few of those include Marlon Brando, Anthony Quinn, Robert De Niro…and Misty Rowe. For some reason, Stella Adler saw something that she loved about me.

Stella opened her famous Studio of Acting in New York City in 1949, but every summer, she would come to teach classes in Los Angeles. But getting into her class was not easy. You had to pass an audition for her, and Stella chose only the very best.

For my audition, I did an intense death scene, and it surprised Stella. She said that she was not expecting something like that from such a young woman. But she said that I was very good and I could join her Studio of Acting. From that day on, Stella Adler became my teacher, my mentor, and my friend. She was one of my dearest friends until the day she died.

Stella was 70 years old when I met her, and she was very elegant. She also encouraged me to dress in an elegant way. She advised me to lower my speaking voice, and once I did that, it led to me landing many more acting roles. I took every bit of advice Stella ever gave me, and she gave me a lot!

Since I hadn't had much education, she told me to read as many books as I could, especially all the great American playwrights like Tennessee Williams. She said I should travel the country and the world if possible, and she took me to Paris to attend an international symposium that celebrated the life of Russian actor Konstantin Stanislavski, whom Stella had known when she was younger!

Why Stella liked me, I will never know. But she really took me under her wing. Stella got invited to the most amazing dinner parties. She knew all the rich and famous people, and for some reason, she liked to bring me along with her. One of her best friends was Steve Allen, and I attended the most wonderful parties at his home.

Stella was so observant. During one of our conversations, she said, "Misty, I don't think you see well. You squint all the time, and I think you should go to an eye doctor." I did, and found out that I was very, very nearsighted. When I put in my new contacts, I said, "Well, this explains everything." All through school, I was told that I was dumb. I wasn't dumb at all; I just couldn't see! They always sat us in alphabetical order and since my name was Rowe, I always ended up in the back of the class, and I could not see the blackboard. No wonder I couldn't answer the teacher's questions.

I studied with Stella every summer, in June, July and August, for 20 years. She was a fabulous teacher, not just to me, but to all of her students. John Ritter, who went on to become a big star with "Three's Company," was in my class. Stella directed me in the play "Waiting for Lefty." As a director, she was very strict, who expected you to know your lines, show up on time and take direction. If you didn't, there would be hell to pay.

Stella knew my weaknesses, and she knew my strengths. The one thing she didn't know during my first year with her was that I was completely broke. I hadn't made my first movie yet, and I had almost no money at all. After I passed my audition to get into her school, I paid half of the bill, and told them I planned to pay the other half in a couple months.

To save some money, I moved out of my apartment and started living in my car. That allowed me to pay for a few more classes. But Stella had an assistant who managed her Los Angeles Studio; her name was Irene Gilbert. She told me I had to come up with all the money or I could no longer attend. So, I stopped going and moved back home with my parents

A couple weeks later, I received a phone call from Stella. She said, "Darling, you have not been to class lately." I explained, "I didn't have the money and Irene won't let me in unless I pay it all." Stella said, "Misty, you are talented and need to be guided. You need to study the great playwrights. You come back to class and I will deal with Irene."

I went back to class and kept going for the next two decades until 1990! And what no one ever knew...until now...Stella Adler never charged another cent. She would never accept any money from me.

During one of our classes, Stella instructed me, "When you are asked to play a dumb blonde...and you will be...never play the character as an idiot. Instead of trying to act stupid, always be childlike. Being like a child with an innocence about the world is much more endearing than playing an idiot." I took that advice to heart and it served me very well, both on screen and off.

If I wasn't with her in person, Stella and I were exchanging wonderful letters. Today, I have 20 years of letters that she sent me. I saved every one. I loved her so dearly. She helped me follow my dream.

In December of 1992, I took my baby girl Dreama to meet Stella. Stella was in failing health and had to use a wheelchair. We took a photo of her as she held my daughter, Stella passed away just two weeks later. As I was writing this book I found this note Stella sent me 45 years ago. It is one of my prized possessions.

Dec. 6, 1975

Dear Misty,

I love and respect you with all my heart, and am sending you some of this love to warm you and make you feel that you belong a little to me...and a lot to the fine work you will do. You have a magnificent talent. Keep beautiful inside and outside.

All my love,

Stella Adler

CHEESECAKE ANYONE?

There is a part of my career that was so absurd. As I look back now, it is so funny. It was my "Beauty Queen Era." I call it my "Cheesecake Era."

While most beauty queens dream of winning the Miss America pageant, my dreams were a little more humble. I had absolutely no money. I couldn't afford a fancy pageant gown, so I decided to enter contests where I didn't need much clothing! Bathing suit contests became my specialty, and I managed to win one after another.

Instead of taking the Miss U.S.A. crown, I racked up such titles as Queen of Queens California, Miss Radiant Radish, Miss Wahini Bikini, Miss Mini Skirt U.S.A, and wait for it…Miss Rigid Tool!

Raquel Welch had been a previous Miss Rigid Tool. The Rigid Tool Company always put out a huge calendar that featured beautiful pictures of bikini-clad girls holding a different Rigid Tool. If you happen to find a 1973 Rigid Tool calendar, for the months of November and December, you will see an 11x14 color photo of me holding a 25-pound portable power drive.

When I won some of those unique contests, I usually got a small amount of cash, between $50 and $100. While the prize money was small, I also won huge trophies. One trophy was so large that each night I shoved it up against my front door. After someone broke into my apartment and stole my TV, I could wedge that big trophy between the floor and the doorknob, to make sure no one could get through the door.

My sometimes-strange pageant career also began in a somewhat strange way. I was still a senior in high school when a friend, Wayne Richter, took my best friend Mary Jo and me to Hollywood. At about 10:00 p.m., we walked (I was barefooted, wearing a miniskirt) down Sunset Boulevard. We passed a man who was selling free press newspapers. When we saw that no one was buying them, as a joke, we told him that we would try selling them. I whispered to my friends, "Maybe this will help me get discovered in Hollywood!" To our amazement, everyone who walked by offered to buy our paper!

A few minutes later, a man walked up and said, "Dear, you should not be doing this on Sunset Boulevard late at night. This is not safe." I laughed, "I want to be an actress. I want to be in show business."

He responded, "Well, this is not how you go about it. You don't stand on the street corner in your bare feet." He continued, "I have a friend and I want you to call him. His name is Charlie See. He is Chinese and he's a photographer, who runs beauty contests. They are all on the up and up, with no hanky-panky. And the girls win money and prizes."

The next day, I called Charlie See, and the first contest I entered was at Myron's Ballroom in Los Angeles. Oddly enough, that's where Marilyn Monroe won her first beauty contest. My first pageant was for the title of Miss Wahini Bikini.

When I signed up for the event, I was told that all the contestants would have to wear a bikini with a sarong wrapped or tied to the top of their bikini bottom. While I had a bikini, I did not have a sarong. I also didn't have the money to buy one, or even the cloth for one. (I told you that we were poor!)

But I wasn't about to let that stop me. I remembered the prom dress that Willie had made for me earlier that year. I also remembered she had a small piece of fabric left over. I found that piece of chiffon material and tied it to my bikini. Since it was so lightweight, it swayed wonderfully as I walked. It turned out to be better than anything I could have purchased in a store.

We had only one mirror in the whole house. It was in our bathroom, and as I looked at myself in the bikini, I thought that I didn't look like most other bathing beauties. I did have beautiful legs and pretty long, blonde hair. But I wasn't very busty. Of course, I knew we had no money for a pushup bra, so I decided to improvise once again.

I got two of my mom's wash cloths, I rolled them up and stuck them beneath the bikini bra. I instantly looked like a totally different woman! As I gazed into the bathroom mirror, my chest seemed to swell with pride!

The Miss Wahini Bikini contest was broadcast on Channel 13. The TV station's most popular show at the time was "Perry Mason," but the Bikini contest also drew big ratings. Gary Owens, who was on "Laugh In," was the host of the pageant, and talk show legend Dick Cavett was one of the judges, so it was a pretty big deal in our local area.

My friend Mary Jo was also in the contest with me. She was standing next to me when they announced that I had won the whole thing! Can you believe that the girl with the little homemade chiffon sarong and two wash cloths in her bikini top won that contest?!

As they handed me a 2-foot tall trophy, Mary Jo whispered, "Your washcloths! Your washcloths are falling out!" Here I was on television, and the washcloths that had been propping me up are now falling out the bottom of my bikini top. Believe it or not, you can see a picture of that exact moment in the photo section of this book. In addition to my trophy, I also won an amazing mink stole…that I put on immediately to cover up my washcloths.

As photographers snapped one picture after another, Charlie See, the promoter, saw a woman standing near the stage. She was smiling from ear to ear. Charlie asked me, "Who is that woman?" I said, "That's my mama. Her name is Rosie." Charlie exploded with happiness. He shouted, "A young, pretty woman with her mama." Then he instructed me, "Take your mama with you, wherever you go, and you will always have a spotless reputation."

As soon as I got my driver's license, I sold the mink stole I had won for $300, and I used that money to buy my first car. It was about what you would expect for $300. It was horrible. It was maroon in color and I called it the "Maroon Goon." I actually bought the ugly, little car before I even had a driver's license, so I let my friend Mary Jo drive us around in it.

During my reign as Miss Wahini Bikini, I made a number of personal appearances, including one in the Santa Claus Lane parade in Hollywood. I wore my bikini as I sat next to Santa. Charlie was proud of me as he watched me on the all-important Santa Claus float. After the parade, he told me I should enter every contest he promoted.

Charlie See looked at the young women who competed in his beauty pageants as "International Ambassadors," and we really were, as he hosted contests around the world. Thanks to Charlie, one of the most memorable trips of my life came in 1970, when I took part in the "Queen of the Pacific Quest" at the Moomba Festival in Melbourne, Australia.

The quest featured beauty queens from the countries that line the Pacific Ocean. Charlie See took me to represent the U.S., since I was from California, and he also took Miss Mexico. We really were ambassadors, as we spent over two weeks traveling to different events throughout Australia. Over that two weeks, I got to know the other contestants from countries including China, Japan, and New Zealand.

My roommate was Miss Mexico, and she was absolutely stunning. She was very wealthy. Every night as we would visit in our room, she would count all her pieces of jewelry before she went to sleep to make sure it was all there. One night she looked at me and said, "You know, in my country, a girl like you would never get to represent Mexico. You have no clothes and you have no money." I looked across the room at the gown I had brought for the pageant. It was my junior prom dress that had been homemade on a Singer sewing machine. I quietly lied, "Well, I'm really just doing this for fun."

And I did have fun, probably more than any other contestant there. I rode in the Moomba Festival parade with Tiny Tim. Tiny was the official grand marshal, since he was very big at the time with his huge hit "Tiptoe Through the Tulips." While I was there, a photographer took photos of me and some of the other queen contestants as we frolicked on the beach. In one of the photos, I was leapfrogging over another contestant. She was Miss Mexico, and that photo ended up going around the world. It ran in hundreds of newspapers. My boyfriend Dennis even saw it in an Asian paper as he served in Vietnam.

The Australian press loved all the beautiful contestants, but for some reason, they really seemed to pay a lot of attention to me. I think it was because, since I was having so much fun, I was always smiling. They also liked the little cowgirl outfit I wore almost every day. Since I didn't have much of a wardrobe, they could usually find me in my cowboy hat and vest. That's what I was wearing the day I was asked to teach the Australian Lord Mayor to go-go dance. As we danced, the newspaper camera flashbulbs were almost blinding.

I charmed the press, but I didn't win the "Queen of the Pacific Quest." Miss New Zealand won that crown. But I did win the Miss Photogenic Award. That award included $500, and I knew exactly how I was going to spend that when I returned to the United States. I was going to the dentist.

Even though I had managed to win numerous beauty pageants, I had always been very self-conscious about my teeth. I had a huge gap in between my two middle teeth, and in my early modeling photos, if you look very closely, you can see that I am putting my tongue up behind my teeth to try to fill in that space.

Every TV or modeling interview or audition I went on, always seemed to end with me being told how pretty I was, but I would need to get my teeth fixed. As soon as I won prize money in Australia, I went to a dentist and had them give me a retainer.

My unique pageant career continued with one hosted by Love's Barbecue restaurant. I didn't win the overall contest, but I was named "Princess of Love", because I had the best ribs!

My ribs helped me get another job with radio D.J. Art Laboe. Art had a rock and roll radio show called "Oldies but Goodies." He hosted an event for all the station managers who aired his show, and he wanted a girl in a bikini to jump out of a huge cake. I had a sash over my chest that said, "Oldies" and on my bikini backside said, "but Goodies."

Since I didn't have my driver's license yet, my mom drove me to the event. When she found out I had been paid $50 and two steak dinners, she said, "This is great! You get all that for ten minutes of work!"

I entered the "Miss Mini Skirt U.S.A." in Los Angeles. Of course, you had to wear a mini skirt, and of course, I didn't have a lot of different clothes to choose from. But I did have a creative mind. In my apartment, I didn't have a door between my bedroom and bathroom. All I had was a long strand of glass beads that you walked through. I cut off a strand of those beads and I sewed them underneath the bust of my outfit, all around and down to the hem of my slip.

During the pageant, as I walked down the runway ramp, all of those beads just swayed beautifully and as I turned right in front of the judges, those glass beads all started clicking together and it almost sounded like they were making music. Everyone was so impressed with my amazing outfit. They had no idea that it was homemade from my bathroom door! That night, I returned home with my magic beads, along with $200 and a huge trophy that said "Miss Mini Skirt U.S.A."!

During one of my pageants, as I was getting ready backstage, I saw a really tall girl across the room. She had dark hair and was very bosomy. I tried not to stare at her, but I was in shock, because she didn't have on a bathing suit. Instead, she was wearing underwear. She was going to go out on stage in just a lace bra and bikini panties that she had dyed hot pink.

As I tried in vain to look away, she breathlessly said, "Hello, my name is Lisa." I answered, all in one sentence, "I'm Misty, why are you in your underwear?" Lisa laughed, "I'm so top heavy that I can't find a bikini top and bottom that fits."

That was the first time I met Lisa Todd. A short time later, Lisa would become a regular on a TV show called "Hee Haw." I had no idea that I would be working with her on that same show a couple years later.

When I think back on my "Cheesecake Era", I just have to smile. Of course, winning something like the Miss America title would have been nice. But I'm just as content with my title of "Miss Rigid Tool.

On June 4th of 1970, I made my first appearance on national television. Bobby Sherman was a huge teenage idol at the time. Bobby was similar to David Cassidy and all the young girls loved him. He was so popular that he had his own TV special on the ABC network.

When I heard they were looking for a girl to be a featured part of a music video in the show, I somehow managed to get a meeting with the show's director David Winters. After we visited, Mr. Winters told me he was going to cast me as Bobby Sherman's "Dream Girl" in the show.

Even though my time on screen was very short, it took a total of three days of filming. And even though I didn't have any lines, since I was on the set three days, David informed me I was now eligible to join AFTRA, the TV union. But when I found out how much it cost to join, I told him I wasn't going to do it, because it would take all the money I was making on the shoot to pay my membership. David shook his head, saying, "Misty, you are paying it. You will thank me years from now. You are young now, but after you join, they will protect you all your life." I listened to David and I joined AFTRA, and he was totally right.

I stayed in touch with David Winters over the next 50 years, until he passed away in 2019. A year before he died, he wrote his autobiography. When he found out I had bought a copy, he told me, "Misty, you have to write your book next. You have to get all of your wonderful memories down, and it's very interesting to go back through your life and see who helped you along the way." Well David, I finally did as you said. I wish you were here to read it.

I enjoyed my time living at the Hollywood Studio Club. During my time there, I always lived with another girl. My first roommate was a nice young woman named Renee Smith. But her stage name was Tara Leigh. I had just started studying acting, and Tara was already on television. She was one of Dean Martin's "Golddiggers" on his network TV show. I thought she was so successful as I watched her pull her new MG into our parking lot and I thought, "Wow, I'm still trying to pay for my teeth retainer."

But at least I was able to park my car next to hers. Of course, it was the old one I bought for $300 when I sold my mink stole. Just before I moved to the Studio Club, my Grandpa Johnson taught me how to drive and that allowed me the freedom to look for a job and to go on auditions.

While most of my time was devoted to attending the Actor's Workshop, I also took on a couple part time jobs. I worked as a French Fry Flipper at a place called Ramone's in Beverly Hills. That might sound like a high-class place, but it was really a McDonald's with a big chandelier. I worked the counter and took orders, but my main job was to cook the French fries. By the end of my shift, I was covered with cooking oil and they called me the French Fry Flipper.

I made $1.75 an hour with no tips at Ramone's, but after a couple months, I heard of a higher paying job. I turned in my French Fry apron and started working for the phone company. As a telephone operator, I made $2.15 an hour!

One day, I was in a coffee shop at "Crossroads of the World", a little area on Sunset Boulevard. I had met another actor from the Actor's Workshop and we were running over our lines as we drank our tea. As we rehearsed, a man came up to me and said, "Hey kid, would you like to be in Playboy? I'll take a picture of you and get you in Playboy."

I was taken aback, and said, "No thank you. I'm an actress. I don't want to do that."

The man responded, "OK, but you've got a great face. If you ever need pictures, you call me." He gave me his card and I saw that his name was Johnny Castano, and he had a photography studio in that area. After seeing that he might be legitimate, I told him, "I don't have any money for photos."

Johnny said, "If I take a picture of your face, would you let me put it in the window?" I responded, "Sure, if you give me a copy of it." With that, Johnny walked away and just as he got out of the door, another man came up to me.

He was a nice-looking man, very demure, nicely dressed, and he asked, "Are you serious about being an actress?" I answered, "Yes I am. I'm studying at Estelle Harmans." He explained, "There are a lot of sleazeballs in Hollywood that prey on young girls, and I'd hate to see that happen to you." He continued, "I have a friend who has a commercial agency. His name is Jack Wormser and here is his number. I will call him and tell him to meet with you. When you call, tell him Noel Blanc sent you."

I didn't know it at the time, but Noel was the son of Mel Blanc, best known as "The Man of 1, 000 Voices." Mel was the cartoon voice of Bugs Bunny, Daffy Duck, Porky Pig, and many others.

I actually walked to my meeting with Jack Wormser, because I didn't have enough money to put gas in my car. But it was worth the walk, because I left that meeting after the largest commercial agency in America agreed to sign me!

After going out on quite a few casting calls and auditions, I finally landed my first big job in an ad for the "FloriGold Grapefruit Company." It was a regional TV commercial, and I played an airline stewardess. As I walked down the plane aisle, I announced, "Coffee, tea or grapefruit." The company liked the commercial so much, that they aired it for 10 years, and I got paid residuals all those years! Today, you can still see that ad on YouTube.

That was the commercial that put me on my way, and I know that it would never have happened without Noel Blanc offering to help me when he first saw me in that little shop. I will never forget his kindness.

Jack Wormser helped get me a lot of TV commercial work in the 70s. One promoted the Yellow Pages, and I appeared in it with comedian Flip Wilson. That spot ran for a long time, and I made quite a lot of money from it.

In 1971, I landed a small speaking part on a network TV special, and that would lead to a very memorable meeting with a musical legend. Comedian Arte Johnson was known for his catch phrase "Ver-r-r-ry interesting" on the "Laugh-In" show. When Arte got his own TV special, it was named "Ver-r-r-ry Interesting."

I was hired for a role that was credited, "Girl in the Gucci Striped Bikini." On the show, I was supposed to walk in and say, "Some men are following me!" Arte did a double take as he looked at me in my bikini, and then said, "I can see why."

Of course, I was comfortable in a bikini, but I found out that for television everything was a lot more complicated. They always like girls in swimsuits to have great tans. These days, on shows like "Dancing with the Stars" they cover everyone with a spray-on tanner. But in 1971, they didn't have spray-on tans, so I had to stand in the make-up room with my arms and legs spread out, as someone took a big, wet sponge and rolled pancake makeup all over me. By the time, they were done, I was dripping all over the place!

They sent me out in the hall to try to dry off, but I was dripping with every step I took. I stopped and stood still, just me in my bikini, with only my fake tan covering me. Just when I thought things could not get any worse, I see an old man, smoking a pipe, walking my way. When he got to me, he stopped, took the pipe out of his mouth and asked, "Young lady, aren't you cold?" I smiled, "It is a little cool out here."

With that, the man took off his jacket, put it around my shoulders and walked away. The show director came out and asked, "Where did you get that jacket?" I said, "From that nice old man." The director laughed, "Well, that nice old man is going to sing on the show tonight. His name is Bing Crosby." So, I can honestly say that the great Bing Crosby gave me the coat right off his back.

In the early 70s, I was hired for lots of television commercials. One of my most famous was for Lincoln Mercury. I was the Lincoln Mercury Bobcat Girl in a commercial that ran just after the Super Bowl.

At about the same time of my first TV commercial, I was hired for my first professional stage acting job. It was for a play called "Lovers and Other Strangers," and it was in Lubbock, Texas. It ran in late December and early January, and that was my first Christmas that I wasn't home with my family. While I was sad over that, I was excited to be making money as a "working actress."

The play took place at "The Hay Loft Dinner Theater." All the actors lived in the hay loft, where we shared a kitchen, and one bath. In the middle of the living room floor was a hydro lift with a square wooden floor. With the push of a button, that would descend straight down to the theater stage. After we finished the play and made our curtain call, the stage would lift us all back up to our hayloft home! It was such a neat place.

But I found out that Lubbock, Texas hadn't seen many California girls. I was washing my clothes at the local laundromat when a woman came up to me and gave me a Bible. She had also written me a note that read, "You're a very pretty girl, but your skirt is too short."

When I came back from Lubbock, I called Johnny Castano, the photographer I had met the same day I met Noel Blanc. I told Johnny I needed a headshot photo to give out at my auditions. Johnny agreed to take my picture, but again, he asked if he could put my photo in his studio window. I told him that would be fine.

Little did I know that Johnny was going to put a huge 3 by 5 foot photo of me in his window. It took up almost half of his store front. A short time later, my phone rang. It was Johnny, and it was a call I will never forget. He told me that a couple had walked into his studio after seeing my photo in the window. He explained that the husband and wife were filmmakers and they wanted me to star in their next movie!

HITCHHIKING IN HOLLYWOOD

Throughout my life, I never smoked, I never drank alcohol, and I never took drugs. But I did do a little hitchhiking.

Ferd and Beverly Sebastian were a cute, married couple who make low budget films. If you went to a drive-in in the late 60s and early 70s, chances are that you saw one of Ferd and Bev's movies. In 1971, the Sebastians were preparing for their latest movie that was called "The Hitchhikers."

To say that Ferd and Bev didn't spend a lot of money on their movies would be an understatement. Their entire budget for 'The Hitchhikers" was $29, 000. That included the salaries for all the actors and promotion for the film. In order to save money, Ferd and Bev did everything themselves, just the two of them. Beverly wrote the scripts and Ferd did all the filming.

The Sebastians had gotten into filmmaking, thanks to a rare California snowstorm. They lived in an area where snowflakes might fall once every 50 years. But one year, a freak snowstorm hit, and Ferd ran out and bought all the film he could afford. Then he went around, taking photos of every house within 5 miles, covered in snow. He had to work fast because the snow quickly melted. Then he made 8x10s of each snow-covered home and went door-to-door, selling them. It was such a rare sight, that every resident bought one. Ferd took all that money and made his first motion picture.

Bev's lead character in her "Hitchhikers" script was a teenage runaway named "Maggie." One day, Bev happened to walk by Johnny Castano's photography studio, where my large picture was hanging in the front window. Bev walked in and asked Johnny, "Who's that girl? We want her for our movie."

When I met with the nice couple, they explained that they didn't have much money. They also asked if I knew any other actors who would work for very little pay. I gave them the names of a number of my friends, including my high school best friend Mary Jo, and I started preparing for my first starring role on the big screen!

We filmed the movie in less than a month. During that time, the small cast and crew lived in two trailers outside Westlake, California. Of course, there was no food catering on this shoot; instead, Beverly made baloney sandwiches for us almost every day.

We filmed all my hitchhiking scenes along busy Highway 101. As cars and trucks sped by, they saw me in my short-shorts and tight, white t-shirt, with my thumb out, acting like I was looking for a ride.

For my month of work, I got paid $1,500, but half of that money was deferred, meaning I only received $750 until the movie was released. I also got a trip to New Orleans to attend the movie's premiere. When Mary Jo and I walked into our room at the Marie Antoinette Hotel, the first thing she said was, "Look, there are two toilets in our bathroom!" I had never seen a bidet before, and I replied, "I guess we can wash our socks in that one."

To promote the film, a local radio station held a "Win a Date with a Hitchhiker" contest. I went to dinner with the young man who won the contest, and then we attended the movie. We had a nice time, but at the end of the night, he wanted the date to continue in my hotel room. I wouldn't let him in, and when he insisted, I had to call the film distributer to come tell the contest winner that our evening was over.

When my parents told me they were going to see the movie, I dreaded what my father might think. I warned them, "This movie will probably not be nominated for an Academy Award, so don't get your expectations up." While I had no major nudity in the film, it was a little provocative. Most of the movie's focus was on teenage girls running around in cut-off shorts and T-shirts, as they robbed the unlucky drivers who picked them up!

I called Mom the day after they went to their local drive-in to see the movie. I asked her, "What was Daddy's response?" Mom whispered, "He spent the entire movie, walking around the car, slamming his fist on the hood."

"The Hitchikers" might not have been my father's cup of tea, but The Los Angeles Times liked me. I received a wonderful review that I immediately cut out to save as the first clipping in my film career scrapbook.

As my movie career was beginning, I was also getting more offers for modeling work. Looking back at my first days as a model, I just have to shake my head and laugh. It was so crazy. I took part in an event called "Lens Clicker Day." Each Saturday, anyone (usually it was all men) was invited to the city park to take pictures of pretty girls. The photographers (anyone who owned a camera) would pay a fee and they could shoot pictures of each young woman. The main reason the girls posed was to get nice photos for their modeling resume, without having to pay for a real photo shoot.

Once I got a little modeling experience, I met professional photographer Peter Gowland. Peter was a "glamour girl" photographer, who had a studio in his house. That's usually a major red flag for any aspiring models, but Peter's wife was always there when we had a photo shoot.

Peter also had a little dog that would sit on a chair next to him as he worked. Seeing that little dog watch me pose, always made me laugh during the shoots, and Peter just kept snapping away. Those photos of me smiling and laughing were always the best ones of the session.

Peter took my photo that appeared on the Rigid Tool calendar. He was also responsible for getting me a lot of work, including a well-paying ad campaign for the PK Ski Company. One of their ads ran as a full page in many different sporting magazines, and featured me wearing their ski boots, while I was in a bikini.

If that sounds funny, you should have seen the photo of me wearing nothing but a Morton Salt box! They made a 5 foot-tall Morton Salt container and then I got inside. It looks like I have no clothes on, but I was wearing a strapless swimsuit that you can't see. The only thing funnier than the picture was the caption they wrote for it that read, "Misty Rowe and her salty box!"

Once "The Hitchikers" was released, I got the attention of a great agent. She was an English woman named Nora Sanders. Nora really believed in me, and she started sending me out on interviews for other TV and movie roles.

But before any of those materialized, I had one more "cheesy title" to add to my resume. I was about to become "Miss Radiant Radish!" The health food store "The Radiant Radish" in West Hollywood was managed by Brian Wilson of The Beach Boys. The store hired me to be "Miss Radiant Radish" as I handed out free samples of the new Gypsy Boots energy bar. Gypsy Boots was a man, whose real name was Robert Bootzin. He was into yoga, fitness and healthy eating.

Gypsy Boots' wife Lois was a dancer. She had put together a group of can-can girls who performed all around the area. When she asked me to join their group, I answered, "Sure I can…can." (I just made that up as I typed this!) Our dance troupe performed at the Pasadena Civic Light Opera, where we did jazz and can-can dances. "America's Got Talent" auditions are held there now, on the same stage where I once danced.

We were booked to do our can-can dance on New Year's Eve at a place called "The Classic Cat." We were warned that as soon as we were finished, "The Classic Cat" would turn into a topless club, with all their topless dancers taking over. We were gathering all our things, getting ready to leave, when a group of police officers stormed in, making a raid. Naked girls ran out into the street as they tried to get away. As topless dancing grew in popularity in the early 70s, my dancing career was coming to an end. Topless wasn't for me. Of course, when you're topless, you don't have anyplace to hide your bosom-enhancing wash cloths!

But I continued my reign as "Miss Radiant Radish," with my main job being to hand out energy bars. My radish costume was quite elaborate. It was the bikini I wore in my high school play, covered in fig leaves. I also added actual radish leaves to it. As I handed out the free samples, I found that a few of the customers were more interested in picking off my leaves. You can laugh if you want, but my "Miss Radiant Radish" job would ultimately lead me to the Academy Awards. Here's how it happened…

A young man walked in and took one of my energy bars. He smiled and said, "My name is Robert." After a quick conversation, Robert asked me out, and I said yes. At dinner, I learned that Robert was a documentary filmmaker. He was very English, and he knew very little about the United States. He was also 12 years older than I, but I didn't care about the age difference. He was very nice and I loved his accent.

During dinner, Robert casually stated, "I have to go to this black-tie event. Would you like to go with me?" I responded, "I only have one dress and it's a pink, short one." Robert insisted, "No, you would need a little, black dress. If you can find one, I will buy it for you."

A week later, I was wearing a little black dress as Robert picked me up...in a limousine. He told his driver to take us to the Dorothy Chandler Pavilion. As we arrived and I looked out the window, I yelled, "Robert, this is not just a black-tie event. This is the Oscars!"

To my complete surprise, Robert was nominated for two Academy Awards! His documentary, "Sentinels of Silence" was about the archeological ruins of Mexico. Orson Welles narrated the film.

I had expected to be sitting in the nosebleed section, but as we were ushered through the audience, we finally came to our seats in the third row. As we sat down, I was surrounded by Hollywood legends.

My parents were watching the awards on TV, and when Robert was announced as a winner, as he got up to receive his Oscar, my mother screamed, "There's our daughter! What's Misty doing at the Academy Awards?!" Robert won two Oscars that night. His documentary was the first and is still the only short film to win two Academy Awards.

After the awards, as Robert was doing interviews backstage, I was "star-gazing," trying to see what big stars I could see. Down the hallway, I spied Hugh Hefner with a beautiful girl on his arm. It was Barbie Benton. Just three months later, Barbie and I would become best friends, as we started working on a little TV show.

HEE HAW

The first episode of Hee Haw aired on the CBS network on June 15, 1969. My dad loved the show. My mom couldn't stand it. When I came home to visit, Mom would roll her eyes, saying, "Oh, he's watching that terrible show again." I think since my father was from Missouri, he related to the rural humor and characters on the show. Little did he know that his daughter would become one of those characters a few years into the series!

Each year, the Hee Haw show added to its cast. It went from less than 10 regulars to more than 25 cast members. In 1972, my agent, Nora Sanders landed me an audition for the show. It was one of the worst auditions I would ever do…and it would turn into the longest running TV role of my life.

After meeting Hee Haw's producer Sam Lovullo, two directors and a writer for the show, I was given a page-long joke to read. Thanks to my great memory skills, I quickly memorized the entire thing. When they gave me the sign to start, I confidently recited everything almost perfectly…until the very last line. It was then that I completely muffed it. I totally messed up the punch line.

I let out a loud squeal as I started to cry, and just when things could not get any worse, one of my contact lenses fell out. I bent down to try to find it on the floor, when Sam Lovullo said, "What a unique and great voice! Can you keep that up?" I smiled, "I have for 20 years."

Sam told me they would be in touch soon, and I went home to wait for his call. But after a few days, I started thinking that I had been passed over. When I called my mom to tell her that I thought I had blown the job, she said, "Don't worry Misty. I am going to pray to St. Jude." She had a little statue of St. Jude and she always turned to St. Jude to "pray for hopeless cases."

Ten days later, Nora Sanders called, saying I got the job on Hee Haw. I immediately phoned Mom, and as soon as I shared the news, she dropped the phone, saying "Hold on." When she came back a moment later, she explained that she had to turn her St. Jude statue around. After waiting a week, she had turned it toward the wall, "to give it a timeout."

A short time later, I was on a plane, heading to Music City. When I landed in Nashville, I met Marianne Gordon and Anne Randall. They were two other "new hires." Marianne would become one of my dearest life-long friends. Anne Randall only stayed with the show for two years, while I would be there for the next 19 years! Gailard Sartain also joined Hee Haw the same season I did.

As we were getting settled into our hotel, the show's creators Frank Peppiatt and John Aylesworth introduced themselves. They said we would start filming the next day, but tonight they would like to show us the town. They took us to Printer's Alley, Tootsie's Orchid Lounge and then we headed to the Grand Ole Opry.

When we walked backstage at the Ryman Auditorium, my eyes were immediately drawn to the most beautiful, glamorous woman I had ever seen. She was sitting on a stool and she had on a lime green pantsuit, covered in sparkles. Her hair was about a foot tall. Yes, Dolly Parton was the first star I ever met in Nashville.

On my first day of filming, I stood behind Roy Clark and Buck Owens as they sang one song after another. My job was to stand on a hay wagon and clap and dance in place, while smiling my biggest smile, and I did that job as well as I possibly could. I clapped, danced and smiled my biggest smile...for six solid hours!

During that time, I noticed that everybody on the set was happy. None of their smiles were fake. They were all having so much fun and were thoroughly enjoying being a part of this wacky show. As I looked closer, I also noticed that everyone was different. Some were skinny and some were fat. Some were beautiful and others were kind of strange looking! Many had gaps in their teeth, and lots were wearing old clothes. And guess what...I felt so at home! I truly fit in with this one-of-a-kind family.

We filmed Hee Haw at the WTVF Channel 5 TV studios. It was very small, and they didn't have enough dressing rooms for everyone. So, they put up shower curtains in the hallway and we stepped behind those curtains to change our clothes. On my first day, as I was getting dressed, a beautiful, young woman opened the shower curtain. She lifted her shirt and yelled, "Flash!" My eyes instantly got as big as her boobs! She laughed as she ran through. I was totally shocked, but Faye Sloan, the show's wardrobe designer laughed, "Oh, that's just Barbie Benton. You can see her in Playboy." I answered, "Well, I just saw a lot of her right there."

You never saw Faye Sloan on camera, but she was such an important part of Hee Haw. She designed all the clothes that we all wore. She was so creative and so smart. She would also become one of my best friends, and we would go on to work together on many, many TV shows and stage productions throughout the rest of my life.

Of course, Hee Haw was known for its corny jokes and its great country music. Since my dad was from the Ozarks, he loved all the country music stars. But like most teenagers in the 60s, I was into the Beatles and Dionne Warwick. But once I started on the show, I quickly became a country fan. After my 19 years on Hee Haw, I spent another 20 in a Patsy Cline production, so country music has always been a huge part of my life.

Being a California girl, it might be surprising that the southern drawl I used on Hee Haw came fairly natural. Dad's Missouri drawl always stayed with him, and I guess it rubbed off on me.

When I first came to Nashville, I didn't know anyone, and I was very shy. Ronnie Stoneman, part of the famous Stoneman Family, and known for her banjo playing on Hee Haw, offered me some confidence-building advice, "Misty, you always say you are so shy, but I don't know why you are afraid to talk to people." She continued, "I was behind you in the gas station the other night. As soon as you pulled in, the entire staff ran out and started cleaning your windshield and pumping your gas. I had to go to the other side and pump my own gas, while they cleaned your car!"

Just a couple weeks after I started on Hee Haw, I celebrated my 22nd birthday on the set. The cast and crew had a party for me, and for Gordie Tapp, whose birthday was also June 4th. From that point on, Gordie always called me his twin. He also called me "Legs," because he thought I had the most beautiful legs on the show. I joked, "But you haven't seen Grandpa Jones' legs."

When I started on Hee Haw, I got paid the AFTRA minimum of $350 a show. But we filmed 13 shows in two weeks, so when I got my first check, it was more money than I had ever made. I knew exactly how I was going to spend it too. I bought a new car. (At least it was new to me.) It was a 1967 Mustang, that was five years old and had thirty thousand miles on it. I paid $3, 000 in cash and couldn't have been prouder as I drove that car off the lot.

I asked my father's opinion on my car and he said it was a good deal. Dad knew a good deal when he saw one, since he had owned a used car lot. It's quite ironic that one of his daughter's most memorable skits on Hee Haw was the one where she appeared in Junior Samples' Used Car Lot, as he told everyone to call BR-549.

As I mentioned earlier, Dad loved Hee Haw from the time it first went on the air. And when I joined the show, he just couldn't believe it. He was the proudest father in the world, and I wanted to be sure to be with him in person when my first episode aired on TV.

We filmed in May and June and those shows started playing in September. I was at my parents' home when my first show was aired. My grandpa was with us and Mom was so excited that she brought in our outside dog so he could also watch me on TV! As the show started, when my picture and name came up in the titles, my entire family just exploded with applause.

During that first show, I was mainly in group scenes, clapping and smiling. But I did get one short skit in the Kornfield. While my mom was not a fan of the show during its first couple of years, she changed her tune the moment I joined the cast. When she saw me tell my first joke in the Kornfield, Mom actually started crying with happiness. As for my dad, in his eyes, it was like I had won the Academy Award. To him, I could not have done anything bigger or more impressive than be on Hee Haw.

During my second year on Hee Haw, I brought my mother to Nashville so she could watch me film. She loved it so much that she flew out again to be with me during my third season. Sam Lovullo treated her so well, and then he asked me, "Misty, why does your daddy never come to see you?" I answered, "He would love to, but he's never been on a plane."

Sam said, "Well, we need to take care of that," and he flew my dad to Nashville, and paid for his hotel room. During one of the tapings, as the Hee Haw Gospel Quartet sang, Sam had my father sit on one of the haybales so he could be seen on camera. It was the thrill of my Daddy's life. And when he watched me play the mechanic in the used car lot skit with Junior Samples, he just thought it was the greatest sketch in the world.

While I spent my first Hee Haw paycheck on my Mustang, I knew exactly how I wanted to use my second payday. I bought my parents a color TV. They had never had a color television before, and they were totally amazed when they saw all the bright colors of Hee Haw.

My brother Bobby also found a small benefit from my new TV fame. He was 16 years old when I went back home to visit. He immediately had me sign a couple sheets of paper. Then he came back and asked me to sign a couple more. When he returned a third time, I asked him what was going on. He exclaimed, "I'm selling your autograph for a buck a piece!"

All my family loved me being a TV "star" on Hee Haw. And over the next two decades, the Hee Haw cast truly became my second family, and those close friendships we made would continue many decades after we stopped filming the show. While Marianne Gordon was the first Hee Haw friend I made, Barbie Benton was my second friend...yes, the same Barbie Benton who flashed me the first time we met! I guess you could say we became bosom buddies!

During my first weekend in Nashville, I was by myself and I asked Marianne if she wanted to go out. She said her husband was coming in but suggested that I ask Barbie. When I called her hotel room, I was surprised when Barbie quickly exclaimed, "Oh yes. Lets go do stuff! I'll rent us a car and drive us around town." As soon as she got behind the wheel, Barbie drove us out of Nashville and to the nearby town of Goodlettsville.

Goodlettsville was filled with many antique malls and shops, and Barbie loved antiques. She really loved them. When she walked into a store, the owners knew they were going to have a profitable day. She would buy and buy and buy. She bought antique clocks, and quilts and rocking chairs. But at the end of the day, I asked her how we were going to get all our purchases back home to California.

Barbie giggled, "Oh, my boyfriend is used to this." She got on the phone and called Hugh Hefner, the founder and publisher of Playboy magazine. I listened as she said, "Hef, I've got the new girl Misty with me. We've been antiquing and we don't know how to get our antiques home." After a quick conversation, she turned to me and announced, "Hef is sending the Big Bunny." I asked, "What's that?" Barbie laughed, "The Big Bunny is Hef's private plane."

I have no idea what it cost, but Hugh Hefner had his pilot fly to Nashville to fill his plane with all this junk! Then Barbie told me, "Misty, cancel your American Airlines ticket, and you can fly back to California with me and all our treasures." As we flew across the country, I couldn't believe that someone who was on Hee Haw was living like this. I knew I was returning home to a little apartment, but I was about to see exactly where Barbie called home.

A week later, Barbie asked me to come over for lunch. I followed her directions to the Holmby Hills. When I arrived at the Playboy Mansion, I found that it was a huge castle, complete with a courtyard and marble water fountain. It was the most beautiful place.

Barbie met me, wearing a T-shirt with no bra and cut off jean shorts. She explained that Hef was gone for the week, and the home was totally quiet. People think of the Playboy Mansion as a 24-hour party, but Barbie was the only person in this huge castle. Of course, she also had a number of butlers and maids on call.

I became very close friends with Barbie. When she got married, I was her bridesmaid, and when I got married, she was mine. She invited me to the Playboy Mansion for many events, with most of those being big buffet dinners, followed by a movie. Many people think the Playboy Mansion was a modern-day Sodom and Gomorrah, but I found that it was actually one of the safest places in Hollywood for a young, single girl. Hef had so much security throughout the complex, that I didn't have to worry about any unwanted advances. I would just go have dinner, enjoy a movie and then head home.

Even though we had completely different lifestyles, Barbie and I were very, very close for about five years. She was in love with Hugh Hefner, and they went together for nine years. But their lives took a dangerous turn when the same group that had kidnapped Patty Hearst also planned to kidnap Hef and Barbie.

I went to visit her in her Nashville hotel room, when I was stopped by heavily armed security guards. Those same guards went with us when we went out to lunch. Barbie eventually left Hee Haw, and she also left Hef when she found out he had been unfaithful to her.

In 1979, Barbie married a real estate developer named George, and they are still happily married today. They have two children and two huge homes, one in L.A. and one in Aspen. Barbie has always been good to me, and I will always love her dearly.

We usually filmed each year's Hee Haw shows in June and October. We shot 13 episodes in June and another 13 in the fall. Then they re-ran each of those. The hours were great, but the pay was not. When I started on the show, my father asked me how much I was getting paid. He was shocked when I happily replied, "$12, 000 a year." Dad responded, "Honey, you can make more than that waiting tables." I answered, "I'm sure I could, but it wouldn't be as much fun."

But each year, I received a $50 raise per show. That doesn't sound like much, but it added up. After I had been there 19 years, I was making $1,200 an episode. The cast also still gets residual money from each time Hee Haw reruns still air on TV today. They're not much, but I still cash the checks!

As the series went on, my role on the show grew each year. While I started out as a pretty girl, clapping and smiling in the background, I started to get more time on camera when the writers created special roles just for me. Those included me singing in the "Gossipy Girls" skit, playing in the "All Jug Band", and appearing with Junior Samples in his used car commercials, and later as his magician's assistant. We also did a similar skit with Junior playing a scientist as I assisted him. For some reason, Junior had a hard time saying my name, so he started calling me "Mipsy." Then he gave me the nickname of "Woman-Child," because he said I looked like a woman, but talked like a little girl.

But my biggest part came when I started doing "Misty's Bedtime Stories." A man named Barry Adleman wrote all the stories and poems I would read in the skit. Barry went on to work with Dick Clark and then Barry became one of the most successful television producers and writers in Hollywood. He has produced hundreds of TV specials like "Dick Clark's Rockin' New Year's Eve," and if you've ever watched any kind of awards show, like the "Golden Globes," chances are, Barry was the man in charge of it.

Barry was a producer of the Hee Haw spinoff show "Hee Haw Honeys", and when that was cancelled, he came to Hee Haw to start writing "Bedtime Stories" for me. We shot the entire year's-worth of "Bedtime Stories" in just one morning. I'd get in the bed and read one story after another. Some of the stories were cute, some were wacky, and some were kind of sexy with double entendre.

Barry had each "Bedtime Story" for me to read off cue cards. But I also tried to memorize each one. I always wanted to get each one right on the first take, because I knew if I messed up, that they would also air that on the show! Hee Haw was known for showing its mistakes or "bloopers" on the show. They quickly found that the mess-ups were funnier than the actual jokes.

Hee Haw became so well-known for its bloopers that we received a special award. Dick Clark and Ed McMahon hosted a popular show called "TV's Bloopers and Practical Jokes." During that show, they gave an award called "The Golden Blooper." I was honored to get to go on their show to accept the award.

If that show had given a "Golden Practical Joke" award, Archie Campbell would have surely won it. He was always playing practical jokes on people. On a number of occasions, when Roy Clark was standing, talking to Buck Owens, Archie would quietly stand behind Roy. Then he would get out his lighter and hold it very close to Roy's rear end. In less than a minute, Roy's overhauls would be almost smoking, and he would suddenly start jumping up and down from the hot bottom Archie had given him.

Another popular Hee Haw sketch was the schoolhouse scene. They originally used real children, but they found their comedy timing wasn't energetic enough, and the skit would be funnier if we used adults dressed as kids. They put George "Goober" Lindsey in a dunce cap, and Kenny Price was so big that he could barely fit into the school desk. Ronnie Stoneman was also in the skit, along with Archie Campbell, who refused to put down his ever-present cigar. Yes, a "boy" with a mustache and cigar was funnier than a real kid. Faye Sloan made me a little pinafore dress, and with my high, little girl voice, I fit right in. Minnie Pearl played the role of our teacher.

My most memorable day in the "schoolhouse" came when I found out that Archie Campbell wore a toupee. I was standing up when Archie came up and "goosed" me. He grabbed my tush and squeezed. I let out a squeal as I slapped the back of his head. My slap knocked his entire toupee over the front of his head, into his face. His lit cigar was in his mouth and it immediately caught his toupee on fire!

I was horrified as a guy came running onto the set with a fire extinguisher. When the small blaze was put out, Archie calmly put what was left of his toupee back on his head. Then he said, "If it was anyone but her, I would be mad." I really thought I would be fired, but instead, Sam Lovullo walked over and whispered, "Misty, Archie has been deserving something like that for a long time. That just added three years to your contract."

I was only a small part of the weekly sketch called "The Moonshiners." That featured two hillbillies who were lazily talking about life, as their bloodhound "Beauregard" slept next to them. In the background, two or three Hee Haw Honeys silently lounged on the porch of a cabin. It always bothered me that the men had all the lines, while the women never got to say anything.

One day, as I sexily posed, barefoot, in my short skirt, "Beauregard" the dog jumped up and came heading toward me. In a flash, he was on top of me, licking and slobbering all over my face, chest and legs. I screamed at the top of my lungs, "Get this dog off me!" But the crew just stood there, laughing their heads off. By the time I had fought "Beauregard" off, I was completely covered in dog spit.

As a wardrobe woman brought me a towel, I yelled to Sam Lovullo, "I am never laying on that porch again! And by the way, the women should have lines to say." That was the day, the Hee Haw writers started adding dialogue for the females in the Moonshiners skit. But I didn't do a lot of celebrating at the time. I had to take a shower.

One of my favorite all-time skits was one I did with the comedy duo Williams and Ree and Lulu Roman. In the sketch, one of the guys played an Indian chief who had tied up a Confederate soldier.

He told him he had the choice of being burned at the stake or he could listen to me sing. I ran in and started singing in my crazy voice, and the soldier told the Indian, "Just light the fire."

People have always asked me if I was using my real voice on Hee Haw, or was I acting. Unfortunately, it was my real voice. It did get lower as I got older, and I learned how to disguise it. But the high pitched "squeak" I had was not put on. Sam Lovullo loved my "squeak" and he used it quite often. When a joke's punch line wasn't all that funny, he'd ask me to throw in my "squeak" after something fell flat, and it almost always made it seem funnier.

While my high-pitched voice worked on Hee Haw, it was a big drawback when I started auditioning for other television and movie roles. After I would read for a part, I was told, "You are very pretty, but your voice is horrible!"

In an effort to lower my voice, I started working with Lee and Sally Sweetland in Studio City. Barbie Benton was going to Lee and Sally to take singing lessons. With their help, Barbie was soon good enough to sing on stage in Las Vegas. And the couple were able to use the same singing techniques to transform my "little girl squeak" into a more normal speaking voice. As an extra bonus, they also helped turn me into a fairly good singer.

Hee Haw had some of the most beautiful, talented and intelligent women on television. While they were mainly known for their beauty, you'll have to take my word for it, that they were also very smart. Of course, all those women wanted as much "face time" on the show as they could get. Each one wanted larger roles, but surprisingly, there was very little jealousy or competition between them.

Instead of trying to hog the spotlight, we each cheered on the others as they did their skits. When Irlene Mandrell joined the show, she said, "I don't know how to act." Sam told her, "It's easy. You just do whatever Misty Rowe does." Irlene and I became friends and I did some events with her and her sisters Barbara and Louise Mandrell. They affectionately called me the "Fourth Mandrell Sister."

As the Hee Haw seasons went on, I became close friends with Lisa Todd, Cathy Baker, Lulu Roman, and of course Marianne Gordon and Barbie. But there was one girl who I did not get along with...

She didn't like me at all, and at times, she made my life a living hell on the set. That woman was Gunilla Hutton. Gunilla was known for her "Nurse Goodbody" character. She had started on the show a couple years before me, so she had seniority. If she didn't want to get up for an early call, she'd tell them to schedule me instead.

I finally went to Cathy Baker, who is the nicest person in the world, and I asked, "Why does Gunilla dislike me so much?" Cathy answered honestly, "I don't know, but you need to stay out of her way." I took Cathy's advice until the day everything came to a head.

They had just come up with the idea of giving Junior Samples an assistant for his BR-549 sketch. Gunilla had talked to one of the writers and got their approval to do the assistant role. They were on the set, and had done a couple takes, when the show's producer, Sam Lovullo, walked in. He immediately yelled, "Cut! I don't know what's going on here, but that role is Misty's."

I will never forget this day as long as I live...they took Gunilla to the dressing room and made her take off the costume. Then they put it on me. I knew that things would now be even worse between Gunilla and me. She left the studio, and Minnie Pearl came over to me. Minnie took me aside and said, "This is not just a regular show. We are a family, and sometimes family members don't get along. You need to try to fix your relationship with her."

A short time later, I approached Gunilla and asked, "Hey, Gunny, have you ever been to a truck pull?" She laughed, "What on earth is a truck pull?" I explained that it was a competition with huge trucks pulling heavy weights. At the time, I was making public appearances at the big arena truck pulls. Before they started, I would sign autographs and take photos with fans, and at the end of the night, I handed out the trophies to the winners. I also told her I could ask the promoter to hire her to sign autographs with me.

The whole time I was talking, Gunilla was looking at me like I was an alien. She was thinking, "This girl is crazy." Then I added, "They pay so much money. I'm making more money appearing at the truck pulls than I do on Hee Haw." Her gaze changed immediately, as she said, "Yes, I would like to try that."

The show's promoter, Buck Beasley, was happy to hire "Nurse Goodbody." As Gunilla and I were walking into the arena, I told her, "There is one thing I forgot to tell you. These things are loud." I handed her a pair of ear plugs just as one of the huge trucks started to roar. Once they got going, it was louder than any drag race and jet on the runway. Gunilla yelled over the engines, "This is excruciating!"

The truck pulls were not Gunilla's cup of tea, and she only did one. But that one event was the start of us slowly becoming friends. When I got engaged, Gunilla surprised me by giving me a wedding shower. She hosted it in her own home. In recent years, we have done many autograph shows and events together. We always look forward to seeing each other and catching up on what has been going on in our lives.

In the early 1980s, I performed with Gordie Tapp at the Hee Haw Theater in Branson, Missouri. My father's side of the family was from Missouri, and before the show, I heard that some of my family was in the audience. During my show, I asked for any of my family members to stand up. I was stunned when the entire first two rows came to their feet. There were two rows of Rowes!

One of those relatives was my Uncle Elbert. He was a poet who taught at the School of the Ozarks. He wrote me the most beautiful letters until the day he died. My Uncle Bill was also there. He lived in Springfield and was a college baseball coach. He was so successful that he was elected to the Missouri Sports Hall of Fame. Years later, when my daughter was born, Uncle Bill and his family drove all the way to California to visit us.

We also did a live concert version of Hee Haw at Knott's Berry Farm. Roy Clark, Minnie Pearl and Roy Accuff were all on the show. My father had always told me, "You are so funny Misty, but you will probably never be much of a singer." When Sam Lovullo found out my dad was going to be in the audience, he came up with a surprise for him.

My father was sitting in the third row, and I walked down the aisle from the back. I was singing in a cordless mic and when I got to Dad, he was still facing the stage. I tapped on his shoulder as I was singing, and he was so shocked that I was such a good singer.

I guess you could call me the rebel of the Hee Haw cast. It wasn't a title I sought out, but once I got it, I carried it as a badge of honor. My first case of rebellion came as we were killing time between takes. I was posed up on top of a hay wagon, and as I looked around the studio, I asked out loud, "Hey, how come there are no black people on Hee Haw?" Everyone just stopped in their tracks. No one said a word, and Gordie Tapp muttered, "This one is from California."

Sam Lovullo told me, "We have Charley Pride on the show." I answered, "Yeah, but he's not a regular cast member." A short time later, when the show was looking for some new Hee Haw Honeys, I asked Sam, "How about a black actress?" He said, "I don't know any." A week later, I put 10 photos and resumes of black actresses on Sam's desk.

A week later, Sam called and said, "Well Misty, I didn't hire any of those women. But I do have some good news. Sammy Davis Jr. is going to guest star on the show." I said, "That is wonderful. I want to tell jokes with him in the Kornfield."

I guess you could call my conversations with Sam "planting seeds" In 1982, those small seeds started growing, as Scatman Crothers became the first semi-regular black cast member on Hee Haw. During our breaks, Scatman gave me tap-dancing lessons in the hallway.

I loved Sam so much. Everybody called him "Papa Sam." He was a big Italian guy who loved parties. He loved Italian food. He loved his wife Grace. He loved baseball, and he loved "Hee Haw" most of all.

Sam was always more than fair with me, but I felt that I needed someone to represent me when I was dealing with not only my Hee Haw contracts, but also my other TV and movie offers. So, I signed with a man named Mike Greenfield. He handled big-name stars like football legend Joe Namath and Dynasty's Linda Evans. His clients called him Greenie and "The Green Machine," because he got them so much green money.

Greenie was the classic big-time agent, complete with a big cigar and calling everyone "baby." He used terrible language and was always running a hundred miles an hour, working on his next big deal.

Then he met Sam Lovullo.

When my Hee Haw contract was up for renewal, Greenie yelled and screamed at Sam, and Sam never flinched. When he told Sam I would leave the show if I didn't get a raise, Sam calmly answered, "Well, we will hate to see Misty go. We will sure miss her."

Greenie called me and screamed, "I can't deal with someone like him! I can't deal with people from the south. I'll get you auditions in Hollywood, but for Hee Haw, you need to get an entertainment lawyer." I found a lawyer who was just the opposite of Greenie. David Rudich was very soft-spoken and I hoped his style would work better on Sam.

After a little back and forth negotiation, Sam still wouldn't give me any big raise. But he did give me the freedom to pursue other television and movie work. He even agreed that I could miss Hee Haw tapings if I had a lead role in a series or movie. He also gave me a car…at least one for the month I was in Nashville to tape Hee Haw.

When I had first asked for my own rental car, you would have thought I had asked for the moon. But I explained that I would fly into Nashville, and when I wasn't on the set, I'd be stuck in my hotel room, with no way to get around town. All the male cast members were given their own rental car. But the 12 females were given just one car that they were expected to share.

Sam agreed to give me a car I could use, but he wanted me to keep it a secret from the other girls. That proved to be impossible when I came rolling into the parking lot in a black Camaro. Because I stood up for myself, the other female cast members eventually got rental cars of their own. But in the interim, they didn't think it was fair that I had one. They also didn't like it when I came in a day or so after everyone else, because I had been working on another project. A few of the other female cast members started doing anything they could to hurt my feelings. One day, as I sat crying in the dressing room, Sam walked in and said, "Don't let the bitches get to you."

Sam was even kind enough to be one of my investors for a production that ran for seven weeks in Los Angeles. I wrote the play called "Just Another Blonde" and it was a big hit at the Callboard Theater in L.A. Sam brought his entire family to opening night. Kenny Rogers also invested in the production.

When I look back at old episodes, it seems that the longer Hee Haw ran, the bigger my hair got! I started out with my natural blonde, straight hair in pig tails. But when the big hair fad of the 1970s came, my hair got a whole lot more complicated.

Since the trend was big hair with lots of curls, I had to start getting perms. Then they would hot roll my hair each morning at 6 a.m. Just before I walked onto the set, they'd tease and spray my hair. Because it was so humid in Nashville, they'd have to do the entire process again during my lunch hour. I would have much rather have been headed to Cracker Barrel, but I never complained.

I think that's one reason I lasted for two decades on the show. I tried to go along with anything that was asked of me. I happily wore any outfit they wanted me to. I said yes to any request, whether it was to take part in a super silly skit, or make some kind of public appearance. I had watched some of the new girls complain about little things and they didn't last long on the show, and I wanted to be around for as long as I could. I think that attitude helped me, not only on Hee Haw, but also throughout my life.

Today, men are almost afraid to give a woman a compliment, but I have never taken offense if a man told me I was pretty. Yes, there were many times in my life, not on the Hee Haw set, but on other occasions, where men crossed the line and came on to me in an unwanted manner. But I let them know that I wasn't interested, and we moved on. I never desired to get someone in trouble or ruin a man's life because he made a play for me.

During my years on Hee Haw, the men were always flirtatious, but that was totally fine. But there was one time when a man crossed the line with me. I was part of the Hee Haw Road Show and we were playing a fair. Before the show, I walked into one of the trailers we were using as a dressing room. Just as I stepped in, Buck Owens jumped out of the back room...with no pants or shorts on.

He did a little dance in front of me and then he went back into his dressing room. I was stunned.

Our wardrobe woman, Faye Sloan walked in and I screamed, "Buck Owens just flashed me with his ding-a-ling!" Faye just laughed and said, "Yeah, it's no big deal...really." We both giggled. That was it. It never happened again. I never tried to sue Buck or get him fired. We moved on. It was no big deal...really.

One of the hardest times for the entire Hee Haw family came during my second year on the show. David Aikman, the comedian who played "Stringbean" on the show, was murdered, along with his wife. They had just returned home from playing on the Grand Ole Opry, when two men who had broken into their home, killed them both.

Stringbean was known for telling his funny stories and playing the banjo. He also played a scarecrow in the Hee Haw Kornfield. His death left us all heartbroken. But it was a feeling we would have to get used to, as we would mourn the loss of so many of our friends. When Junior Samples passed away in 1983, Billboard magazine ran a photo of Junior and me together. On August 4, 1987, Kenny Price died of a heart attack, when he was just 56 years old. Unbelievably, just three weeks later, Archie Campbell also died from a heart attack.

We said goodbye to Minnie Pearl, Grandpa Jones and Roy Acuff. In March of 2006, my phone rang. It was a reporter from CNN, asking for my reaction to the death of Buck Owens. That's how I found out Buck had died. I was heartbroken.

I was also devastated when the Hager Twins, John and Jim died within a year of each other. The Hagers loved my teenage daughter, and they would call her up just to tell her jokes and make her laugh. The one bad thing about having a big "family" is that you have to tell so many wonderful people goodbye.

YOU MEET THE MOST INTERESTING PEOPLE IN THE KORNFIELD

Hee Haw was known for corny jokes and great country music. During my two decades with the show, I was blessed to work with hundreds of amazing country music stars. From the newcomers to the biggest superstars, every country artist wanted to be on Hee Haw. Here are a few of my memories of a half dozen of those true musical legends.

Loretta Lynn – I loved Loretta Lynn. She did our show many times, and I got to tell a lot of jokes in the Kornfield with her. We always used cue cards, and since Loretta was far sighted and I was near sighted, we had quite a time trying to read our lines.

On one occasion, Loretta was supposed to say the word 'toupee', but for some reason, she couldn't say it right. We would jump up from the Kornfield and she'd read her line until she got to 'toupee', and she'd pronounce it 'to pee' and we'd have to go back down and start all over. We went up and down at least a dozen times, and then we started giggling and couldn't stop. Finally, Loretta just gave up. She yelled, "Well who the heck would wear one of those anyway?" All of us immediately turned and looked at Archie Campbell.

Conway Twitty- Loretta's singing partner was also a regular guest star on Hee Haw. Conway was such a huge superstar. He probably didn't need to do the show, but he came on just because he enjoyed being there. He loved performing, but he also liked to tell the jokes and have fun with all the cast. I was so young when I started on the show, that I really didn't appreciate his greatness. But as the years went by, I began to realize what an amazing talent and huge star he was. Conway Twitty also came on our "Hee Haw Honeys" spinoff show. Loretta did too. The Oak Ridge Boys and Statler Brothers were also frequent guest stars on both shows.

Willie Nelson – The first time I saw Willie on Hee Haw, I couldn't believe a male country singer had longer hair than mine! But I got to know Willie a little bit over the years. My husband Barry produced one of Willie's concerts at the Tropicana in Atlantic City, and we got to visit with him backstage. And when Hee Haw was honored at the TV Land Awards, Willie came and sang for us.

Dolly Parton – Dolly was the first person I ever met just after I came to Nashville. I visited with her backstage at the Ryman Auditorium the night before I started filming Hee Haw. During the time she was opening for Kenny Rogers, I got to see her quite often as I attended many of Kenny's concerts. But it didn't take long for her to get so big that she wasn't going to be opening concerts for anyone. I talk in depth about my friendship with Kenny in "The Gambler" chapter of this book.

Johnny Cash – Johnny Cash was larger than life. He was a superstar and legend. And I was blessed to become friends with Johnny and his wife June. Like Conway Twitty, they sure didn't do Hee Haw because they needed the exposure. Everyone in the world knew and loved them. But still, Johnny and June returned to the show each and every year, and sometimes twice a year. And I was thrilled when Johnny made an appearance on our "Hee Haw Honeys" show. The very first song I sang on the show was an old June Carter tune called 'No Swallerin' Place.' In between songs and jokes, June and I would visit, and she was always such a hoot.

Johnny did a big TV special that was billed as his salute to the women of country music. I was honored to get a big part in the special, as I performed with June and Minnie Pearl. June was very funny and when they hired me, they told me I got the job because they wanted a funny female who could match June's humor. They also let me wear my own favorite red dress during the show's finale.

Minnie Pearl – I was so blessed to get to work with Minnie on hundreds of occasions. The Johnny Cash special was the first time I did my impression of Minnie in front of her, and I was so relieved when she loved it. We went on Hee Haw road shows together, and I played her niece on a special country music episode of "The Love Boat." When my parents came to the Hee Haw tapings, Minnie always took time to pose for photos with them.

I've written about Minnie quite a bit already, but now I'd like to share the best advice she ever gave me. I had just joined the cast and wasn't used to being a TV "star." During a break, as I was running to change outfits, a young man stopped me in the hallway and asked for an autograph. I scribbled my name on a piece of paper and gave it back with a rude, "Here."

Minnie Pearl was watching the entire time, and she followed me into the dressing room. As only a true friend will do, she bluntly said, "Young woman, don't you ever treat a fan like that again. If you do, you won't have many fans left." She continued, "When someone asks for your autograph, take some time with them. Ask their name, and where they're from. Giving someone 30 seconds of your time won't hurt you, and they will remember their moment with you, for the rest of their life."

I never forget Minnie's words, and from that point on, I always treated my fans in a way that I think would have made Minnie proud.

You could always find great country music stars on Hee Haw. But there were many very interesting, non-country performers who visited our show. Here are a few who I thought I would never see in the Kornfield.

Sammy Davis Jr. - Oh, I adored Sammy. He came on the show and I got to do jokes with him. He sang with Buck and Roy, and then they put him in the Kornfield with us gossipy girls. He was standing next to me as I went to hit the high note in our song, and he actually put his finger in his ear. He said, "I have never heard a sound like that before."

Ethel Merman – We were surprised when Ethel came on. She wasn't country and wasn't used to sitting on a hay bale. But everyone was real excited to have her there. I was walking down the hall as Ethel was coming out of her dressing room, and I approached her with, "Excuse me, Miss Merman, but I just love how you sing. I want to be like you someday." Ethel answered, "Oh yeah. Well, let me hear you. Sing my song, 'There's No Business, Like Show Business." And right there in the hall, I started singing her signature song.

But after just a couple lines, Ethel slapped me on the back and said, "Honey, you've got to be a lot louder than that! You've got to project." And then she started singing, "There's no business, like show business...." At the top of her lungs. You could hear her voice echoing throughout the entire TV studio. I thought, "How many people get a singing lesson from Ethel Merman?' I guess there really is no business, like show business!

Ed McMahon – Johnny Carson's sidekick loved Hee Haw. He came to visit the set anytime he could, even if he wasn't on the show. He just loved being around everyone and he was fun to be with. In addition to the Tonight Show, Ed also hosted a show with Dick Clark. The show was called "TV's Bloopers and Practical Jokes." Ed was such a fan of Hee Haw, that he showed lots of our outakes and bloopers on his show, and then the Hee Haw Honeys were invited to come in person to be on their show. While we were there, they gave us their "Golden Blooper Award."

Billy Carter – When Jimmy Carter was President of the United States, his brother Billy was almost as famous as Jimmy was. Billy was a true good ole boy. He ran a gas station and loved beer. He became so popular that they named a beer after him, and when he came on the show, he brought cases of his Billy Beer for all of the men and he brought big bags of Plains, Georgia peanuts for all the women. I got to joke with Billy in the Kornfield and he was really a lot of fun.

Leslie Nielsen. – Leslie was a wonderful actor and comedian. His greatest fame came in the silly "Airplane" and "Naked Gun" movies. And off screen, Leslie was just as silly. He loved to make fart noises, and he carried a whoopie cushion everywhere he went. Leslie and I did numerous celebrity golf tournaments together. He looked kind of out of place on Hee Haw, since he didn't sing, but everyone still enjoyed having him visit Kornfield County.

John Ritter. – John was the son of country singer Tex Ritter. John lived in the shadow of his father until he got the lead in the TV series "Three's Company," and that show helped make John Ritter a superstar. I knew John quite well before he came on Hee Haw, since we had been in the same Stella Adler acting class. John was always friendly and kind. He loved country music and he enjoyed being on our show as much as we enjoyed having him there.

Will Geer- Will Geer was in hundreds of TV shows and movies. But he will forever be known as Grandpa Walton on The Waltons. Will was one of my all-time favorites. He came on Hee Haw and sang songs with the cast, and they put me next to him for most of those. When a guest star came on, I was usually picked to stand behind or beside them because I was always so animated and smiling as I sang and clapped.

When we took a break for lunch, most of the cast left to go eat at Cracker Barrel. I was getting ready to go, when I saw Will Geer sitting by himself. I asked if he was going to lunch and he said he didn't have a car. I asked him if he'd like to go to lunch with me. I told him I usually ate just vegetables and he said, "Let's go! I love vegetables." We went to a little café and when we got back, he said, "Now Misty, I'm going to give you my number, and I want you to call me when you get back to California, I will take you to lunch to return the favor.

Almost as soon as I got home, I called Will and he had me come have lunch with him on the set of "The Waltons." All their cast ate outside on a picnic table and I got to meet all of them as I had lunch with Will.

Will was planning to come to my house to help me plant tomatoes. But he passed away before we could get them planted. He was a lovely, lovely man.

Jonathan Winters – Jonathan was a comic genius. The creators of Hee Haw, Frank Peppiatt and John Aylesworth, had worked on The Johnathan Winters Show before they came up with the idea for Hee Haw. So, they invited him to guest star on their show.

Gailard Sartain had really been looking forward to it, because everybody always told him he was like a young Jonathan Winters. So, he got to meet his hero. But I got to do a skit with Jonathan and it was one of the most difficult things I have ever done!

Jonathan was known for his ad-libbing. He just made up stuff and it was always crazy and funny. But on Hee Haw, we relied on cue cards. We didn't ad-lib very much at all. But when they held the cue cards up for Jonathan, he would go off into some kind of other land and make things up a mile a minute. He would talk about nonsensical things. I was standing there, waiting to say my line, but I never got to, because Jonathan never stopped talking all of his gibberish!

I tried to be patient and kept silently telling myself, "This is Jonathan Winters, a comic genius." But as it went on and on, I began to think, 'This is kind of stupid.' They let the cameras roll on him for more than an hour, and I think they got just one joke that they could use on the show. It was an experience I will never forget! Ironically, a photographer for Newsweek magazine was on the set that day. They took a picture of me and Jonathan together, and it ran in the next week's issue of Newsweek. I'm so glad they happened to get a photo when I was smiling, and not rolling my eyes! Yes, you do meet the most interesting people in the Kornfield.

In 1978, the creators of Hee Haw decided to create a spinoff show. It was called Hee Haw Honeys. The new series was based in a truck stop and would star Lulu Roman, Kenny Price, Gailard Sartain and Kathie Lee Johnson, who would soon become nationally known as Kathie Lee Gifford. The producers were also searching for someone to play Kathie Lee's sister on the show. I found out about their search in a very unique way.

I was in a store in Hollywood called "Trashy Lingerie." I was trying on lingerie and when the woman in the dressing room booth next to me heard my voice, she asked through the wall, "Are you Misty Rowe? I just tried out for your part?" I asked, "What do you mean?"

She explained that they were auditioning girls for "a Misty Rowe type" role. Of course we didn't have cell phones back then, so as soon as I got back home, I called Sam Lovullo up. I said, "Sam, I was trying on underwear today, and I heard the craziest thing." I asked him why they were looking for a "Misty Rowe type," but they didn't ask the real Misty Rowe. He said, "We need someone who can sing." While I was no singing star, I could hold my own, singing with the cast, and the very next day, Sam hired me to be a lead character on Hee Haw Honeys.

Barry Adelman, who had written my "Misty Bedtime Stories" on Hee Haw, was the main writer on Honeys. Kenny Price played my dad and Lulu Roman played my mom. That was kind of strange since Lulu was only 5 years older than I. Lulu and I grew very, very close during that time.

Hee Haw Honeys had so many country music legends come on for guest appearances. Those included The Oak Ridge Boys, Conway Twitty, Loretta Lynn, The Statler Brothers and Jerry Reed. But the best thing about the show was our star billing! While Roy Clark and Buck Owens were the main stars of Hee Haw, on Hee Haw Honeys, Lulu, Kenny, Gailard, Kathie Lee, and I were the stars.

But just as Sam had explained, my character was expected to sing, so now the time had come for me to prove that I could. When he scheduled me to do a solo, I met with the great songwriter Shel Silverstein. Shel had written "Boy Named Sue" for Johnny Cash and "One's on the Way" for Loretta Lynn. Shel said I should sing an old June Carter Cash song called "Ain't Got No Swallerin' Place."

I took Shel's advice and my song turned out so well that Sam Lovullo came up afterward and said, "Get three more songs ready to sing later this season." In the middle of my second song, one called, "Gonna Get Along Without You Now," Gailard Sartain came up behind me, wearing bright red lipstick, with two pigtails and an apron. He was imitating me as I sang, and when I finally noticed him, I grabbed a mop and chased him around the set. Everyone loved it so much, that they left it all in the show that aired.

Hee Haw Honeys ran just two seasons, and it was its success that ironically led to its downfall. The show usually came on before Hee Haw in most markets, and when the ratings came out, the Honeys' ratings were very strong, but Hee Haw's seemed to lose ground. To make sure viewers didn't suffer from Hee Haw burn out, the Honeys were cancelled.

While my starring role only lasted a year, my star was still on the rise. In 1983, I was asked to pose for a poster. Farrah Fawcett's poster had made her a superstar, so I jumped at the chance, and my poster sold over a million copies!

While Farrah wore a skin-tight swimsuit for her famous poster, I wore a pair of my own shorts that I had worn for over a decade. And here's something you never heard…those shorts had actually belonged to my brother!

Back when I was 18, I came home and my little brother Bobby was throwing out some worn out jeans that didn't fit him anymore. He was 13 years old. When I saw him tossing them in the trash, I said, "I'll take those."

I washed them and then I cut them off to turn them into shorts. I embroidered lace and little beads and flowers on them. Then I wore those little jean shorts when I filmed the movie "The Hitchhikers." I wore them during the entire movie, and I continued wearing them on Hee Haw. After I posed in them for my poster, I put them in a drawer for the next decade.

After the birth of my baby, I figured I would never be able to fit into those shorts again, so I was going to throw them out. My friend Joan Kovats was with me and said, "You can't do that! Those are worth a lot of money." She asked if I would donate them to the "Broadway Cares" charity auction. I handed them to her and laughed, "No one is going to want my old shorts." But I was wrong. They sold for $3, 000.

While somebody has my shorts, another person has one of my bras. Noel Blanc's wife Katherine asked me to take part in a fundraiser for cancer research. They asked celebrity women to make a bra. I used some material from a pair of my Hee Haw overhauls to make mine, and they auctioned it off.

I don't know who owns my shorts or bra, but I do know who's sleeping in my bed...my co-author of this book, Scot England, was such a big fan of mine that he bought the bed that I used for all of my "Misty's Bedtime Stories" on Hee Haw. Scot also helped Lulu Roman with her book, and when I found out that he owned my bed, I knew he would be someone I would like to work with.

HAPPY DAYS

Since we taped the entire year of Hee Haw shows in just a couple months, that allowed us a lot of time to work on other projects. In early 1974, I was planning to spend most of the year directing a live stage production of "The Apple Tree." Cyndee, a friend from high school, was going to make all the costumes for the production. Our plan was to make it a touring show that we would take to country clubs and mobile home parks.

But my "mobile home park dream" had to be put on hold when I landed a role on one of the most popular shows on television. That show was called "Happy Days," and I would play the part of Wendy the Car Hop. "Happy Days" premiered on ABC on January 15, 1974. I wasn't in the show's first episodes, but when the series was picked up for its second season, I got a call to read for their casting director Bobby Hoffman. I drove to the Paramount lot where I met Bobby and one of the show producers, Bill Bickley. Gary Marshall got most of the publicity for producing the show, but Bill was also a producer.

Bill was on a golf cart, and as soon as Bobby told him I could do the job, Bill said, "Jump on, we've got to get you to wardrobe!" As I got on the cart, I asked, "I'm starting now?" Bill laughed, "You sure are!" As he wheeled us through the lot, he explained, "You are really saving us. We had hired a girl, but she cancelled at the last minute."

When we got to the wardrobe department, they had me try on a short blue skirt, a white blouse and white boots and a little hat. As I modeled the outfit for Bill Bickley, he said, "I want that blouse tighter."

The wardrobe lady said, "If I make it any tighter, the buttons will burst off." Bill responded, "That's what I want. I want the character to look like the buttons are going to burst off her shirt."

Once I slipped back into my own clothes, which were highlighted by an almost as tight T-shirt that read "Hollywood," I was taken to meet the other cast members, Ronnie Howard, Donny Most, Anson Williams and Henry Winkler. Since my shirt was so tight, when I held my arms at my side, you couldn't see the letters 'H' or 'D'. When I noticed Ron Howard staring intently at my chest, he blushed, "What is 'Ollywoo'?" Everyone laughed when I held my arms out to reveal the word "Hollywood." I knew I was going to fit right in with these guys.

When the show debuted, Ronnie Howard was supposed to be the main star. Henry Winkler's role as "The Fonz" barely appeared and seldom spoke in the first episodes. His role was so small that he was not even listed in the opening credits. But by the second season, "The Fonz" had become the surprising breakout superstar of the show, and Henry Winkler was on his way to becoming a TV legend.

I was signed as a recurring regular for eight shows. I had numerous speaking parts in that season, but the best thing was that they used me in the title credits at the opening of the show. As the show has aired continually in re-runs, for the past 45 years, people have watched Anson Williams as "Potsie" grab "Wendy the Car Hop" and give me a huge kiss. Then I take a huge banana split and throw it all over his chest. And every time they play that show opening, I get residual money in the mail!

People always ask me what Ron Howard and Henry Winkler were like. The answer is they were both incredible. The entire cast was. Of course, Ronnie had been a child star as 'Opie' on The Andy Griffith Show. Now, he was the star of another program that was going to be the number one show on TV. He could have been stuck up and full of himself, but he wasn't. He was very down to earth and quite shy. He drove an old VW to work, and his dad was his manager.

It's hard to describe just what a huge star Henry Winkler became during my time on Happy Days. Off set, Henry wasn't at all like the character he portrayed, Arthur Fonzerelli. That just showed what a true actor he was. But he did have a couple things in common with "The Fonz"…they were both very cool, and they both loved "chicks."

Henry kind of took a liking to me and one day he asked me, "Do you like music?" When I replied, "Of course," he said, "Well over lunch, I'm gonna sit in my car and listen to music. Why don't you come and sit with me?" I told him I was headed to makeup to have my hair done. He said, "Well, I'll wait for you."

While I was in the hair unit, I told the stylist, maybe she shouldn't put curlers in my hair, because Henry wanted me to listen to music with him in his car. The stylist laughed, "You know that Henry asks every new pretty girl to listen to music with him in his car?"

So, I stayed inside and got my hair done. But Henry never held that against me. He was always so helpful as he gave me great acting advice. He watched me do one scene and afterward, he said, "Boy, you don't have time for anything, do you? You just ram through the scene a mile a minute." Then he instructed me, "Why don't you pace it? Slow it down. It will seem more natural and you'll get more time on camera." It was great advice and I became a much better actress because of Henry.

In the 70s, every young girl, and many women, had a crush on Henry. I was no different. My crush for him became even greater when I went back to my job at Hee Haw. I was thrilled when I received a large envelope in the mail and saw that it was from Henry. I couldn't believe it when I looked inside and found a handwritten poem that Henry had written about me. He called it "Mist" and it was written on the back of a page from his own Happy Days script. It was such a wonderful gift that I have saved it all these years. You can read it in the photo pages on this book.

Henry also gave me a gift in my favorite Happy Days episode. The show was called "Guess Who's Coming for Christmas." It's a very sweet and poignant episode. In the show, "The Fonz" gives Wendy a heart necklace, while Donny Most as Ralph Malph tries to kiss me under the mistletoe.

I did a lot of scenes with Donny Most, I guess because Ralph was always trying to win over Wendy. Donny was always funny and a joy to work with, and now, almost unbelievably, more than 45 years later, I am working with Donny again, and he is still a joy. You'll read much more about that later in this book.

Donny was in my famous banana split scene that they used in the show's opening. I often get asked how many banana splits I had to throw on Anson Williams during that scene. Luckily, we did it in just one take. First, we did a couple run throughs, practicing how he would grab and kiss me, and then I just acted like I was throwing the desert on him. But Jerry Paris, the director, warned us that when the cameras rolled, we all needed to do everything perfect the first time.

And we did! Everyone was so relieved that no "Take 2" was needed. It would have taken Anson Williams a long time to cleanup and do it all again. He was a sticky mess.

One of my most memorable episodes was called, "Not Making of a President." My big scene was during a presidential rally, when Wendy jumps up on the stage, wearing a trench coat. She says, "It doesn't matter who you vote for. The important thing is that you vote, vote, vote!" Then I took off my coat to reveal a pink, 1950s one-piece bathing suit. Yes, I will admit that bathing suits were a big part of my career!

People remember me from that small moment I was on screen in my swimsuit. But I remember that episode, because it was one of the first things that Ron Howard ever directed. Jerry Paris was the show's main director, but when he found out that Ron's real dream was directing, he became Ron's mentor.

During this episode, Ron learned that one of the director's jobs was to approve all the costumes. Of course, my costume for this show was a swimsuit. I was wearing it under my trench coat when I heard a knock on my dressing room trailer door. It was Ron and Jerry. But Ron was so shy that he kept looking at the ground. Jerry hit Ron's elbow and said, "You've got to look at her to make sure it's authentic. Ask her to take off the coat."

Ron blushed as he whispered, "Misty, would you mind very much just opening the coat so I can see the suit?" I didn't mind at all, and I knew this whole thing was more painful for him than it was for me. I opened up my coat and showed Ronnie my swimsuit. He quickly diverted his eyes as he said, "That's fine, that's perfect." Ronnie was just the kindest, sweetest guy, and I am always very proud that I can say Ron Howard directed me.

Marion Ross played Ron's mother Mrs. Cunningham on the show. I really liked Marion. She also was a student of Stella Adler's, as was Henry Winkler. I just loved everyone who was a part of Happy Days, and it was so exciting to be on one of the most popular primetime network shows. To make things even better, I was still able to stay on Hee Haw, which was the highest rated syndicated TV show in America. No matter how busy or popular I got with my other film and TV work, I never once thought about leaving Hee Haw. It never entered my mind. The Hee Haw show and cast had become my second family. It was like home...a home I never wanted to leave.

But things were pretty busy, and they were about to get even busier. 1974 and '75 were the craziest and most exciting years of my acting career. In '74, I filmed the first half of the Happy Days season in the springtime. In June, I went to Nashville to tape Hee Haw. I was back at Happy Days in the early fall and then in October, I was back to Hee Haw. In the middle of all this, I got the lead of Marilyn Monroe in the movie "Goodbye, Norma Jean."

Just when things couldn't get any more hectic, I got a call from Mel Brooks, asking me to audition for the lead role in a new TV sitcom he was producing. That show was called "When Things Were Rotten." I'll go into much more detail about that in just a bit. But I will say that I passed the audition and went on to film the series pilot episode. After the ABC network picked it up as a series, I knew that something would have to give. There was no way I could do three TV series at the same time.

As I've said before, I would never consider leaving Hee Haw, so that left only one option. I would have to say goodbye to Happy Days. When it came to my bank account, there really was no question of which way I should go. How much did I get paid for Happy Days? A whopping $325 for each show! That's it. Of course, the big stars like Henry, Ron, Anson and Don all made much, much more. So, when Mel Brooks offered me $1, 500 a show, plus lots more in overtime, I didn't think twice.

I looked forward to the next exciting chapter of my life. But I knew I would miss my Happy Days friends. It would be years, and sometimes decades before I met many of them again. I didn't see Henry Winkler again until 2006, when we both were attending a gala in honor of Stella Adler.

30 years had passed since Henry's invitation for me to listen to music in his car with him. I knew he had enjoyed quite an exciting life since then, and I wondered if he would even remember me. I was so happy when I found him to still be the same warm and wonderful man he had always been. I introduced my husband Barry to him and as Henry took my hand, he looked at Barry and said, "Oh Barry, I had such a crush on this woman!"

If I ever find myself needing to smile, I only have to think back to the year 1974. For me, those truly were Happy Days.

GOODBYE, NORMA JEAN

From the time I was in high school, when I talked with someone for the first time, they almost always said, "There is something about your voice. You sound like Marilyn Monroe, because you have that same breathy quality in your voice."

When I got to Hollywood, one reviewer said, "She looks like Marilyn Monroe and she makes as much sense as Gracie Allen." I found that I landed more parts if I used my high-pitched, squeaky voice for funny roles, and then used my breathy, Marilyn voice for sexier parts.

In late 1974, I auditioned to actually portray Marilyn in a movie called "Goodbye, Norma Jean." The film centered around Marilyn's early life, mainly as a teenager, and up to her early twenties, when she changed her name from Norma Jean Baker to Marilyn Monroe. At the time, I was 24 years old, and the movie producers thought I was too old for the part.

They interviewed hundreds of Marilyn lookalikes, but couldn't find one they liked, so they finally granted me an audition. Before I went, I hired a photographer to take photos of me dressed as Marilyn. I even wore a Marilyn wig, and when I saw the final black and white pictures, I was shocked that I looked like her. My favorite was one of me in a white dress with one of my shoulder straps falling off.

I took the photos with me to my audition, but I dressed in cut off shorts and a tight sweater. I had my own long, curly hair and wore no makeup, only lip gloss. I wanted to look as young as possible. I was sitting in the waiting room when the director, Larry Buchanan, walked through. He did a double-take when he saw me and asked, "Who are you?" In my best breathy Marilyn voice, I whispered, "I'm Misty Rowe." He smiled, "Come in here!"

My plan worked to perfection. The combination of my current, very young and innocent look, along with the photos of me as a mature Monroe impressed them enough to offer me the job! I was about to become the very first woman to ever play Marilyn Monroe in a motion picture.

Before we go any further, I need to say…if you've never seen "Goodbye Norma Jean," please don't! Please, please don't. To say the least, it wasn't the Marilyn Monroe movie I had envisioned. One of my best friends went to see it in the theater and the next day she called and said, "Oh my God, Misty. You were raped or molested in almost every scene!"

Am I proud of that film? Absolutely not. During the filming, at the end of almost every day, I went home and cried myself to sleep. During the filming, they kept changing the script, adding new scenes. Almost every addition called for me to take my clothes off. I was very intimidated, and I very reluctantly complied with almost everything that was requested of me.

But things just got too wild for me. It was getting too sexual and too explicit. One day, they said we were going to rehearse a scene, but they secretly had the cameras rolling. A man jumped on me and started ripping off my clothes. I started screaming and crying. There was no acting; it was a real assault, and they just kept filming.

I finally got to the point where I had to stand up for myself. One morning, when I walked onto the set, I was met by a very buxom, scantily clad woman, who was wearing stiletto heeled leather boots and carrying a long whip. When I asked who she was, the director informed me, "We've written a new scene. You are going to be on a bed, and she is going to be whipping you."

I replied, "Oh, no she's not." I walked to my dressing room trailer and slammed the door. Larry Buchanan tried to talk me into coming out, but I said I wouldn't until that scene was cut. Larry asked, "What am I supposed to do with this whip?" I laughed and said, "Do you really want me to tell you where to put it?"

A major part of the "Goodbye Norma Jean" movie centered around the infamous "Hollywood Casting Couch," where many careers were made, and many were lost. When I came to Hollywood, I had already heard about the powerful TV and movie men who promised to make stars of women if they slept with them. I received many of those offers, but that was a line I would never step over. I may or may not have become a bigger star if I had, but that was something I was just not willing to do. I think I ended up working enough and had a good enough career without spending time on "the casting couch."

The most degrading part of "Goodbye Norma Jean" came during the very last shot. The script had me saying the line, "That is the last time I'll ever get on my knees for anyone." I filmed the line and did a good take. But then the director said, "Let's try that with a new line." The new line was much more crude; something I would never say out loud. I refused to say it. "When I approved the script, I never agreed to say something like that." The director sighed, and said, "That's a wrap, everybody."

Little did I know, that after I finished my filming, the director brought in a Marilyn sound-a-like and she recorded the new, very crude line he wanted. Then they dubbed that over my scene and did their best to match her words with the movement of my mouth. They never told me about the change. I would find out about it in a very public way.

The best thing about the film was the movie poster. It featured a huge, full body picture of me. Even though the entire movie centered on Norma Jean's early years, the poster's picture was me as the older, very glamorous movie star Marilyn.

The one bright spot about "Goodbye Norma Jean" came once the filming was over, as it gave me more publicity than I ever got in my entire life. Since I was the first actress to play Marilyn Monroe in a film, the press from around the world wanted interviews and photos of me. The media demand was like nothing I had ever experienced. On Hee Haw and Happy Days, I had been part of a group of people or large cast, but now I was the one and only person with the star billing all to myself.

After my horrible experience during the shooting, I wasn't very interested in promoting the movie. But my contract called for me to do promotional appearances for the film, as long as the producers agreed to pay all my expenses. And they paid to send me around the world for a year and a half. In all honesty, I'm sure the producers spent much more on promoting the film than they did in actually making it.

Our first stop was the Cannes Film Festival in France, where I received a quick lesson on how some movie producers operate. When I went to check into my hotel, I was met by an Australian man who was one of the main producers of our film. He escorted me to my room, which also happened to be his!

I refused to step inside and told him I would sleep in the lobby. I went downstairs and was sitting on my suitcase, when a handsome young man named David Blake introduced himself. He was English, but also lived in New York. I explained to him why I was preparing to spend the night in the lobby. Then he turned to speak in French to the people at the front desk. In just a few minutes, he was able to get me my own room.

I fell almost instantly in love with David. While my Cannes schedule was packed, we arranged to take a quick trip to Paris together, and at the end of the festival, as I got ready to go back home, we promised we would see each other as often as possible.

The movie producers wanted to play me up as "the second coming of Marilyn,' so I always wore a Marilyn wig, and made sure to give every interview in my best sultry, Marilyn whisper. Every reporter wrote, "She is the same height as Marilyn, and she has the same Marilyn smile and even the same ivory skin." Then they would ask, "Are your measurements the same as Miss Monroe?" Again, in my Marilyn voice, I would ad-lib, "Oh, I will never tell."

Flashbulbs popped when I met Arnold Schwarzenegger, who was promoting his movie "Pumping Iron" at the festival. Arnold was big, but I was a bigger hit with the press. The photographers went totally crazy for me. I stayed in a beautiful hotel on the beach, and every time I stepped out of my room, twenty or more photographers were waiting to take my picture. I never let them down, as I changed from one evening gown and sexy dress to another. When one of my short walks turned into a paparazzi free-for-all, I couldn't help but laugh, when I looked over to the nearby beach, where a dozen bare-bosomed women were suntanning. But every photographer ignored the nude women, so they could take pictures of me…with my clothes on!

I was the hit of Cannes. But the photographers would get one last photo-op that I hadn't planned on. After sitting through the first screening, when it came to the very final scene, I watched in horror at the newly-dubbed-in last line. I couldn't believe it. For a few seconds, I sat in total shock. Then as the lights started to come up in the theater, I ran out.

All the photographers, waiting in the lobby, grabbed their cameras and started snapping. The next day's headline was "Marilyn Flees." When a photographer asked the movie producer why I was running, he quickly lied, "Oh, she just realized she had forgotten to put on her underwear."

But I attended the movie opening in Australia. I traveled to premieres in Italy and London, and showings all over the United States. At one point, I was flying 15, 000 miles a month.

My life really changed during that time. The movie itself didn't make me a "star," but I became a pretty big celebrity because of all the press interviews and promotion I did for the movie. But being known as "Marilyn Reincarnated" also became a little overwhelming. She was such an icon, and her persona started to overpower my life. I didn't want to go around wearing a blonde wig, being an impersonator. I was an actress and I wanted to be myself.

While I found that I had a very huge following of Monroe fans, and I still do today, I never had any desire to revisit my time as the movie legend. But that didn't stop another major motion picture from being made.

In 1988, Larry Buchanan, the director and producer of "Goodbye, Norma Jean," wanted to do another film about Marilyn. In the 13 years since the original movie, I had become well-known for "Hee Haw" and many other TV and movie roles. When Larry asked me to star in "Goodnight, Sweet Marilyn," I turned him down, saying I was not interested at all. I forgave myself for making such a horrible mistake early in my acting career, but now that I was older, I would not repeat such a mistake.

I never thought about "Goodnight, Sweet Marilyn" again...until 1989, when I received a phone call from a representative of the Screen Actors Guild. They asked, "Misty, have you seen this new movie? It's 80% you throughout the film." I couldn't believe what I was hearing.

"Goodnight, Sweet Marilyn" opens with an older actress portraying Marilyn Monroe in bed in the hours before her death. As she drifts into unconsciousness, her life flashes before her. And for over an hour's worth of flashbacks, they used all the footage of me in the original "Goodbye Norma Jean"! It was unbelievable.

They used all my old footage without my permission...with no pay whatsoever! I did not get paid a cent for "Goodnight, Sweet Marilyn."

The SAG official asked what I wanted to do. I was pregnant and my doctor was warning me to limit my stress, so I told the Actors Guild I would think about it. A short time later, I lost my baby. I called SAG back and told them, "I am in a haze right now and I don't want to go through a court litigation." I know I should have sued them, but I didn't. I just let it go.

I never speak about "Goodnight, Sweet Marilyn." It is all too painful.

ELTON AND MARILYN'S DRESS WITH A LOBSTER BIB

Elton John first released his song "Candle in the Wind," which many people call "Goodbye, Norma Jean," way back in 1973. The tribute to Marilyn Monroe was on his "Goodbye Yellow Brick Road" album. But the song didn't become a hit in the U.S. until the late 1980s.

When we were filming the movie "Goodbye Norma Jean" three years after Elton's original song, I thought we would for sure use the song in the opening titles of the movie, and it should have been used throughout the film. I mean, if you were going to name the movie that, why on earth wouldn't you use the song? But they didn't.

Elton's manager wanted the movie producers to pay $60, 000 to use the song. But the film had such a low budget that they couldn't pay that amount. I was heartbroken that we didn't use Elton's song. But I was thrilled to meet Elton himself as I was promoting the film.

In 1976, I traveled to England for the premiere of "Goodbye, Norma Jean." On my first day in London, all the press followed me to a city park. I posed for all of the photographers, and they wanted me to strike every glamorous pose I knew. After about a half hour, I noticed a little boy, skateboarding in the park. I walked over to him and said, "That looks like fun." He asked, "Would you like to try?" I kicked off my high heels and said, "Sure!" As I hopped on the skateboard, the paparazzi started clicking away, and that is the photo they ran in the next day's paper. They scrapped all the glamorous photos and used the one of me on a skateboard! The next day, the newspaper headline read, "The new Marilyn Monroe skates into London."

The movie flew me in a week and a half early to promote the opening. And promote it I did. Each day I was there, my picture appeared in almost every newspaper and magazine in England, as reporters and paparazzi followed me from one event to another.

That night after my skateboard photo appeared in the local newspapers, I attended the Tin Pan Alley Ball. It was an awards ceremony for English musicians. I wore the most beautiful white dress. It was the only Halston designed dress I ever got to wear. I was having dinner, enjoying the awards, when a tall, gorgeous young man approached me. He introduced himself as Michael Hewitson, and said he was Elton John's personal assistant. Michael said, "Elton would like to meet you." I said, "Sure."

As Michael walked me across the room, I stopped and picked a rose out of a vase that was on a table. I wanted to have something to hold in case I got nervous as I talked to Elton. I never knew what to do with my hands when I got nervous as I spoke to people.

I followed Michael to the table and Elton stood up to shake my hand as Michael told him, "Elton, this is Misty Rowe. She is the Marilyn Monroe girl you saw in the paper." Elton said, "I saw you riding the skateboard and I hoped I would be able to meet you while you were in London. When I saw you tonight at your table, I told Michael, 'That's the girl!'"

I found Elton to be quite shy, and of course, I was as well. I looked down at the rose I was holding, and on the spur of the moment, I gave it to him. As I did, the newspaper flash bulbs went off by the hundreds. They lit up the entire ballroom. The next day's paper featured our photo on page one, with the caption, "A Rose for Elton."

As soon as he saw the photo, Elton asked Michael Hewitson to call me. Michael explained that Elton had tickets to the musical "A Chorus Line" for that night. I was expecting him to ask me to go with Elton, but he surprised me by saying, "Elton can't be there, but his mom and dad are going, and he wants to know if you will go with them in his place."

I told Michael I would love to go, and he said they would send a car for me. I informed him that I had a very full day of fashion shoots and media interviews, with my last stop scheduled for the famous Madame Tussauds Wax Museum, where they wanted me to stand next to their Marilyn Monroe wax figure.

After posing all day, I knew that it was about time for me to go to the musical, but the manager of the wax museum whispered in my ear, "You know, we have Marilyn's dress from "The Seven Year Itch." We have her real dress. Would you like to try it on?" I said, "Sure!"

He went and got the dress, and I found that it was a perfect fit. We were taking photos of me in the dress when the car with Elton's parents pulled up. I said, "Oh, I am late for this event," grabbed my purse and ran out to the most beautiful white Rolls Royce.

Michael Hewitson was driving the Rolls and we all headed for the theater. After enjoying 'A Chorus Line', we all went to dinner, but in the middle of the meal, Michael started looking closely at me, and he asked, "Is that Marilyn's dress? Her real dress?" I said, "Yes, it is. I didn't have time to change at the museum." Michael yelled,

"Waiter, get us a bib!" He was in a panic, "You cannot get anything on that dress! I can't believe you are eating in Marilyn's most famous dress." I had to finish my meal, wearing the biggest lobster bib I have ever seen.

After dinner, he took me back to my hotel. As I was saying goodbye to Elton's mom and dad, two Lloyd's of London security guards stepped up to our car. Another gentleman was with them and he said, "Miss Rowe. You left with Marilyn's dress, and we want it back." They took me by the elbow and walked me to my room, where they waited outside my hotel door while I took off the dress.

Looking back, I sure am glad I didn't spill anything on that dress. In 2011, it sold at auction for $5,000,000! They probably could have gotten more if they had included a lobster bib with it!

That trip was the beginning of a lifelong friendship with Michael Hewitson. When Elton purchased a home in Bel Air, California, Michael stayed there to watch over it while Elton was away. His move from London to California allowed Michael and me to become great friends. He became my escort to many events and he was the perfect shopping partner for me. He has a sense of style and fashion that I did not have.

There was one particular dress in which Michael and I had a very memorable disagreement. I was shopping for clothes in Hollywood and I saw this incredible red, sequined dress. It looked like a sparkly red mummy. It was the most wonderful dress I had ever seen. Before I paid a pretty high price, I called Michael and asked him to come look at it.

He drove over and as soon as he saw the dress on the mannequin, he loudly stated, "Oh, my God! That is the tackiest dress I have ever seen! You cannot wear that! It's the worst thing I've ever seen."

But I persisted with, "Just let me try it on before you say 'No'."

As I stepped out of the dressing room, Michael stood in awe, saying, "You have to buy it. That was made for you. It is absolutely beautiful."

I now call that my "infamous, red dress," because I wore it everywhere I went. If I had a movie opening and important party, you knew you would see me in that dress. I wore it so much, that Marianne Rogers told me, "Are you wearing that again? Well, I'm giving you a fox stole so you can cover it up with something."

That red dress helped me land a big part in a Johnny Cash TV Special. Johnny was doing a salute to the women of country music. I was in the running to do a comedy routine with June Carter Cash and Minnie Pearl. Whoever they hired would also be in the show's big finale when all the women would be dressed in beautiful evening gowns.

Faye Sloan, who was the wardrobe designer on Hee Haw, was also working on Johnny's show. When she overheard them saying they didn't have money in the budget to get another evening gown for the finale, Faye stepped in and said, "Misty Rowe's got her own evening gown. She never leaves home without it!"

When Michael Hewitson saw me on the special, he said, "I told you the first time I saw that dress on the mannequin that it was a showstopper!"

In 1978, I got to visit with Elton John again when he hosted a birthday party for Michael at his Bel Air home. I took my boyfriend Dave Rowland. Dave was totally star struck and asked if we could get a photo with Elton. Knowing how private Elton is, I worried that he would say "No." But he didn't mind at all, and you can see it in the picture section of this book.

I would have loved for Sir Elton John to have made an appearance on Hee Haw. Can you imagine him in the Kornfield?! I think he would have had the time of his life and he would have looked great in a pair of our overalls.

Michael Hewitson now lives outside of London, and we are still in touch. He is a dear friend and I have loved him for many, many years. Since I've talked about him quite a bit in this chapter, I thought it might be fun to let him write a few of his memories of our time together:

"Since I was eight years old, I had a passion, and almost obsession with Marilyn Monroe. When I was 13, I was at the London airport when Marilyn arrived to film "The Prince and the Showgirl." She smiled as she walked past me. The next day she waved at me from her hotel window. A Life magazine photographer took a picture of that exact moment.

So, in 1976, I was very excited when I read that "The Second Coming of Marilyn Monroe" was going to be in London. The moment I met Misty Rowe, I fell head over heels in love. That might seem odd, coming from a gay man. But meeting Misty was a total thrill for me, and I was even more thrilled when we became great friends.

For years, we have been soul mates. We've shared wonderful times together. I was also at her side through boyfriends, marriages, and health issues. And I could always count on her to council me through my own tribulations.

Yes, Misty Rowe had a very strong resemblance to Marilyn. But she is so much more than that. To me, she is a beautiful and talented lady...and a true friend."

-Michael Hewitson/ Personal Assistant to Sir Elton John

MAID MARIAN MUGGED

The mid 1970s were some of the most fun and exciting times of my life. Ironically, I was about to star in a TV series called, "When Things Were Rotten."

The great actor and producer Mel Brooks saw my picture in People magazine and called me in for an audition for the new series he was producing. When I arrived at Paramount Studios, I first met with Norman Steinberg. He was also a well-known producer, who had worked with Mel Brooks on the movie "Blazing Saddles."

After passing my interview with Norman, he said, "I want you to meet Mel. But you are so pale. I don't think you will live another day because you are so pale." I told him, I tried to stay out of the sun as much as possible.

When I heard that the series was a parody of Robin Hood and his Merry Men, I thought I would try to dress the part for my audition. I wore a long gown, with a beige cape and I put flowers in my hair. It was how I thought Maid Marian would dress.

In the People magazine photo that Mel Brooks had seen of me, I had been dressed as Marilyn Monroe. Now, as I walked in to meet him, I looked like a totally different person. But he must have liked what he saw. When he got his first glimpse of me, he stood up in the middle of this room full of TV executives, put his hand out to me, and said, "Shall we dance?" And I danced with Mel Brooks. He looked into my eyes and said, "Do you dip?" I giggled, "Of course." As he lay me back in a dip, everyone in the room laughed and applauded.

After our interview, on my way out, Mel said, "Misty, thanks for dressing for the part." Without pausing a moment, I answered, "Well, I wasn't going to come naked."

That was the first of nine interviews and auditions I did for that role! There was so much competition to get a starring role in a Mel Brooks series. But after nine interviews, I got that plum role! I was hired as the only female regular in the entire cast of "When Things Were Rotten." Most of my cast members were TV veterans, some already well-known and a few would soon become very big stars in different series.

One of those was Bernie Kopell. Bernie had been on "Get Smart," and would soon become very-famous as Doc Bricker on "The Love Boat." I enjoyed working with Bernie and he was always a gentleman. He also helped me when one of my married male co-stars started flirting with me a little too much.

My dressing room trailer was right next to this "over friendly" actor and he was always saying, "I will come over to your trailer at lunch." Bernie told me, "I'm taking care of this right now." At our break, the man walked up to the steps of my trailer and yelled, "Honey, are you there?" Bernie was inside and he held a white hankie out the door and said, "Come on in sweetheart!" That was the last time I had an unwelcome visitor for lunch.

Dick Van Patton was also in the cast. Just a year or two later, Dick would become the star of his own series called "Eight Is Enough." I was surrounded by all the older men, and I was quite young and shy, but they were all so nice to me. That series was such a training ground for me. I had worked with amazing comedians on Hee Haw, but now I was working with these totally different Mel Brooks comedians, and it gave a real boost to my career.

While I was thrilled to meet Mel Brooks, I was truly in awe when I met his wife. Mel had married Anne Bancroft in 1961. She was one of my heroes. Anne was one of the great acting talents of our time. She was one of the very few people to win an Oscar, Emmy and Tony Award. When I heard Anne would be attending the screening of the pilot of our series, I couldn't wait to meet her.

But sometimes, things don't always go the way you had dreamed.

During the screening, I watched as Anne sat next to Mel. I planned to go talk to her as soon as the lights went up. But when the show was over, as people came up to congratulate me, I saw Anne coming down the aisle toward me. I tried to stay cool.

She got to me and then coldly looked me up and down, as she sneered, "My God, you are young." And she kept walking! That was our entire conversation. As I watched her leaving, I thought, "Yes, I am young."

After having the weekend off, when I got back to the set on Monday, Mel came up to me and said, "Misty, I have to apologize for Anne. She always thinks I'm in love with my leading ladies." I said, "Oh, that's alright."

But then I was shocked as he continued, "And that's why she didn't invite you to the cast party." I asked, "A cast party?" He said, "Yes, we screened the pilot, we had the cast party. I'm sorry you weren't invited, but my Anne gets so jealous." So, Maid Marian, the one and only female star of the show, didn't even get to go to her cast party.

On "When Things Were Rotten," I had to talk totally different than I did on Hee Haw. Mel told me he wanted me to talk like a "British Marilyn Monroe." I said a few lines in my breathy Marilyn voice, and he said, "Now, just give it a little more Brit."

"When Things Were Rotten" was supposed to be based back in the time of Robin Hood, so one of the things I enjoyed the most about the series was the period clothing we wore. The wardrobe manager took me to Western Costume, where they had made all of the classic costumes for films like "Gone with the Wind" and for stars like Elizabeth Taylor.

They measured and fitted me for the most beautiful gowns, made of the nicest satin and fabric. Mel Brooks wanted my clothes to be beautiful as he instructed me, "I don't want you to walk into the room. I want you to float into it." They made me a pair of leather boots by hand and each boot had 100 laces. It took a half hour each morning for the wardrobe lady to put them on me.

Even though the show was a comedy, Mel wanted all the scenery and costumes to be as authentic as possible. I wasn't allowed to paint my fingernails because "They didn't have nail polish in Robin Hood's day."

Of everyone on the set, including all the actors, the people I became the closest with were those in the wardrobe department. They were always working so hard to make sure I had the perfect clothes and that they all fit me perfectly. I was also very close with my hair and makeup people. They spent a lot of time getting my hair just right, and each day I would have to be at the studio by 6:00 a.m., so they could start the long process of getting me ready. I was usually on the set 4 to 5 hours before I ever stepped in front of the camera.

One of the reasons I enjoyed working for Mel Brooks so much, was because he let me wear more clothes than anybody ever had! I showed quite a bit of cleavage, but other than that, I was always covered in wonderful dresses throughout the entire series.

Dick Gautier played Robin Hood. Dick was known for his handsome good looks and had been on lots of TV shows. Mel Brooks also brought in the most amazing guest stars each week. The great songwriter and actor, Paul Williams was a guest. During our down time on the set, Paul sang me little bits of different songs, and when he got really bored, he started a conga line around the studio. He yelled at me, "Come on Maid! Get in our line!"

It seemed that every week, I got to work with a new, fantastic comedian. Comic legend Sid Caesar was a guest star. This would be the first of a number of times Sid and I worked together. English actor Dudley Moore also guest starred. He came on the show just before he hit it big on the American movie screen. Dudley's "When Things Were Rotten" show was my very favorite episode of the series.

Dudley Moore might have been the guest for that week's show titled "Wedding Bell Blues," but it also put me in the biggest spotlight I had ever been in. Mel Brooks wrote the episode just for me, and the entire show centered around my character of Maid Marian getting married to Dudley Moore. Dudley was just hysterical in the show and it became one of the highlights of my career.

The episode was so important to Mel, that he paid to fly Marty Feldman in from London to direct it. Marty was known for playing Igor in Mel Brooks' film "Young Frankenstein." He was also known for his bulging, crossed eyes. Before he arrived, Mel pulled me aside and whispered, "Now Misty, you know about Marty's eyes. You need to know this before he gets here..." I leaned in, knowing he was going to tell me something very serious. Then he said, "If you ever want to hide from Marty, just stand right in front of him."

I made a number of public appearances as we promoted the series. During one of those, John Travolta would save my life. Well, maybe not my life, but he probably saved my career.

In January of '76, I was asked to do a telethon at a TV station in Grand Island, Nebraska. The telethon raised funds for the United Cerebral Palsy Association. John Travolta, who was on his way to becoming a superstar, was also on the telethon. John was taking the world by storm with his character of Vinnie Barbarino on the series "Welcome Back Kotter." But he hadn't filmed "Saturday Night Fever" or "Grease" yet. James Drury, from the western "The Virginian," was also on the telethon.

When my plane landed in Grand Island, the wind chill temperature was 40 below zero. I knew right then that I would not be wearing any bikini during this appearance!

When we got to the station, we found out that we weren't going to just come out and say a few words and then leave. All of us, me, James Drury and John Travolta, were expected to work six hours in front of the TV cameras during the telethon. By the time it was over, we were doing everything we could to entertain the viewers and get them to call in with a pledge. We tried to show off every talent we had...and a few we didn't.

John did some dancing, though it was nothing like the moves he would later show in "Saturday Night Fever." At some point in the night, a viewer said they would make a large pledge if I sang a song. I had been taking some singing lessons, but I was not singing publicly yet...especially on live TV.

But the telethon host came up with the idea of telling viewers that "Misty Rowe will sing a song live, if you can raise this much money." I was instantly terrified. I felt bad that I was silently praying that the telethon would not raise any more money!

But the calls kept pouring in and the total continued to rise. I went to the band to see if they could play something I knew. We came up with the old Judy Garland song, "You Made Me Love You." So, there I was. Totally unrehearsed…and unnecessary. As soon as they started playing, I knew it wasn't even in my key.

I started to sing (kind of), "You made me love you…I didn't want to do it…I didn't want to do it." That's for sure. I didn't want to do it! Either the band was playing too slow, or I was singing too fast, but in between notes, I could hear that the phones had stopped ringing. The viewers weren't calling. I knew they were at home, sitting speechless, stunned at what they were witnessing. I silently hoped that "The Virginian" James Drury would come in and shoot me. If I was a horse, he would have put me out of my misery.

The Virginian didn't ride to my rescue, but John Travolta did. John ran on stage and grabbed me. He signaled to the band to speed up, and he started singing the song with me. And for the next couple of minutes, John Travolta sang "You Made Me Love You" to me! His oh-so-kind gesture made me love him forever.

I got a lot of publicity from the "When Things Were Rotten" series. Every magazine and newspaper interview or story about the show always included a picture of me, front and center in any cast shot. But the most press coverage I received during the show, came in a very odd way. Before it was all over, the New York Times would run the headline, "Maid Marian Mugged by Woman in Gotham."

All the craziness started when I decided to go to see my boyfriend at the time, David Blake. David was in New York City, and I was excited to visit the Big Apple for the first time. While I was visiting him, I went shopping at Bloomingdale's. After shopping, I went to the store's ladies' room. I put my purse down on the floor to wash my hands, and a woman came from out of nowhere and shoved me against the wall. My head hit the wall hard and I slid down to the floor, as the woman went through my purse until she found my wallet. She took it and ran out of the bathroom.

I started screaming and a store clerk came in. I explained what had happened, and instead of running to try to catch the robber, the clerk yelled at me, "You don't leave your purse on the floor in New York City!"

When I got back to David's apartment, I had no identification and no money. He said I should go to the Paramount Pictures New York City office and explain everything. I did and they called a photographer to take a new I.D. photo for me, and they were able to get me an advance on some of my residuals from my "When Things Were Rotten" Series.

I was thankful for all the help they gave me. But the next day, I was shocked to see the photo they had taken of me in the New York Times newspaper! I didn't plan on telling my parents what had happened to me, since I didn't want them to worry about me being in the big city for the first time. But that photo and story got picked up by the Associated Press, and it ran in every newspaper in the country. Within a day, all my friends from California to Texas to Nashville had all read about me being mugged.

The press just ate it up. Every paper ran the same story, but each one tried to top the other with the headline they wrote for it. One said, "Maid Marian Finds New York Rotten." Another read, "Maid Marian Should Have Called Sheriff of Rottingham."

I lost the money I had in my purse that day. Soon, I would lose all the money I was making on that TV series.

110

"When Things Were Rotten" was canceled after only 13 shows. One of the main reasons for the cancellation was the show's high production costs. Mel Brooks was used to making movies that had huge budgets, and he continued to spend like that on the TV show. While most sit-coms, including "Happy Days," had just one soundstage, ours had four. Paying our large cast and crew and flying in big-name guest stars also added to an always growing production expenses.

I shall forever miss my Merry Men. But at least I can still see them on DVD!

PLAYBOY

It was a trip to the meat market that I will never forget.

I stood at the meat counter as my favorite butcher wrapped up a couple chicken breasts for me. For some reason, he wasn't his normal, jovial self, and I thought something might be up when he didn't ask how I was doing. Finally, as he gave me the total, he whispered, "I saw a picture of you in a magazine, and I didn't think you'd do anything like that."

I asked, "What picture and what magazine?" He answered, "It was a men's nudie magazine." I drove straight to the closest bookstore and found the magazine he was talking about. It had a topless photo of me. I was sick. Yes, I had disrobed for a number of my films, but I had agreed to those occasions that only lasted for a second or two. But I did not OK any magazine photo.

My agent told me there was nothing I could do about the severe invasion of my privacy. But my friend Barbie Benton said there was something I could do.

Barbie had posed for Playboy magazine numerous times. Of course, her boyfriend Hugh Hefner was the owner of Playboy. Barbie told me, "The only way to stop those bad photos from surfacing is to put some beautiful ones out there yourself. You need to be in Playboy."

It seemed so easy for Barbie to take her clothes off for the camera, but it was not easy for me. It was just not something I was comfortable with. But I told Barbie I would have my agent contact Playboy. (I secretly advised Nora Sanders to make so many demands and ask for so much, that there was no way they would say "Yes.")

Nora asked for more money than any of the playmates received. She also asked that I get complete approval of all the photos (something that Barbie never had). I also wanted the photo shoot to be at my home, with a female photographer. Much to my surprise, Hugh Hefner said "Yes" to everything we asked.

In the spring of 1976, they did my photo shoot in my home in Laurel Canyon. I came out in my robe so the lighting guy could set up all the lights. But I wouldn't take my robe off until he went out to sit on the porch. Suze Randall, Playboy's first female photographer, took the photos over two days. She brought wine and strawberries on the second day. I told her I didn't drink wine, but she said, "You will today. You were so awkward and shy yesterday, that we can't use any of those photos. We need to loosen you up today."

Then they asked me to come to their studio to shoot a few more photos, because Hef had a special surprise for me. Since I had played Marilyn Monroe in "Goodbye Norma Jean," and since Marilyn had been the very first cover girl for Playboy, Hef had come up with an idea. He owned the original red velvet backdrop that Marilyn posed nude on back in the 1950s, and he got it out of storage and had me reenact her famous pose. So many years had passed since Marilyn's photo shoot, that the red velvet had faded and was now more orange than red.

Once all the pictures were taken, Marilyn Grabowski, one of the editors at Playboy, called me. She said, "Misty, your "Star Pictorial" is ready, but I wanted to get your thoughts on something." She explained that if I was in the October issue, I would get six pages of photos, but if I was in the November issue, I'd get only four pages. I said, "Well, if we're doing it, shouldn't we do the six pages?" Marilyn said, "Maybe not in this case. The November issue is going to feature a very long interview with Jimmy Carter who is running for President. That's why we have to cut back on some of our photo pages, but we are expecting it to be one of our biggest selling issues ever."

So, I went with the four pages of photos and they ran in the, now very famous, Jimmy Carter Playboy. In that interview, the soon-to-be President admitted to "lusting in his heart." The issue sold out everywhere and is now one of the most sought-after Playboy magazines. So, I guess if you were going to be in Playboy, that was the one to be in.

While I didn't get many photo pages, I was surprised that Playboy also ran a multi-page article on me. One of their writers interviewed me, and fought for the longer story, saying, "She's just not a nude model. She's a real actress." He not only interviewed me, but he also called my acting teacher Stella Adler. I'm sure she was surprised to get a call from Playboy, but she said some very nice things about me.

I got paid a lot of money to pose for just a few photos for Playboy, and I used that money to buy a bigger home. Thanks to that larger home, I was able to take in and take care of my grandfather until the day he died.

When my issue came out, my Catholic mother, who said the rosary every single day, went out and bought 20 copies for me to sign for her friends. I knew if it was OK with Mom, then I had no worries. Now, as I look back at those photos, (which I don't do very often) they seem so innocent. I didn't really show that much skin, and it's really nothing compared to what you can see in almost every magazine and all over the internet today.

I have a couple more interesting stories about Hugh Hefner. Hef hosted a special screening for my movie "The Man with Bogart's Face" at the Playboy Mansion.

As usual, I drove my old 1967 Mustang. I gave the keys to one of the valets as I got out at the circular courtyard in front of the mansion. At the end of the evening, I had to wait almost an hour for the valets to return my car. I found out that they didn't want an old car like mine sitting in front of the mansion, so they drove it to the other end of the property and parked it in a field.

As I waited, James Caan, who was known for starring in "The Godfather," came out and asked what kind of car I had. I told him a '67 Mustang. (Of course, this was now 1980.) James laughed and correctly predicted, "Well, wait ten years, and your car will be considered a classic."

But I was embarrassed by the incident and I decided that I would spend my next movie earnings on a car that was so extravagant that they would be proud to park it in front of the mansion. I did exactly that, when I bought an automobile that was 30 years older than my '67 Mustang! I bought the most beautiful 1936 Cord Roadster. It was a convertible, with a white top and burgundy body.

I bought the car from Marianne Rogers' decorator. I totally fell in love with that car. It stole my heart. It was my lucky charm and I went to all my auditions in that Roadster.

116

On another occasion, I was asked to sing at one of Hugh Hefner's birthday parties at the Playboy Mansion. They wanted me to sing Marilyn Monroe's song, "Diamonds Are A Girl's Best Friend." I said, "I can't sing that song! I don't know it." But the party planners somehow arranged for the famous Mel Tormé to give me singing lessons. I asked, "Mel Tormé? The Velvet Fog?"

Hef's parties were always so elaborate. After actor James Caan did a funny bit with a saxophone, I came out in a white Marilyn Monroe dress to sing my song. Record producer and songwriter Berry Gordy played the piano for me, and thanks to Mel Tormé's lessons, I somehow got through the song, and Hef loved it.

How many people can say that their posing in Playboy led them to having Mel Tormé teach them to sing?

WORKING ACTRESS

During the 19 years I was on Hee Haw, I also acted in many other TV shows and movies. Since Hee Haw was syndicated, and not a primetime network show, I was allowed to do many other TV projects. If I had been on ABC or NBC, my acting roles would have been much more limited.

Some people think all I ever did was pop up out of a Kornfield, but I actually had a pretty busy, and successful career. I've covered my TV series "Happy Days" and "When Things Were Rotten" in other separate chapters of this book. But here are a few of my memories from other parts I played:

In 1972, the same year my first movie "The Hitchhikers" came out, I also appeared on the Doris Day TV show. I only had a couple lines as I played a newlywed. Doris was very nice, and she loved animals. She had a little gift shop where she raised money for her animal-related charities. I still have the Christmas ornament I bought in her shop almost 50 years ago.

A year later, I was in a couple episodes of "Love, American Style." I don't remember anything about those, but I do remember my three appearances on "The Dating Game." The first time was just after I won my Miss Wahini Bikini title.

My first time on the show, I was the woman asking questions of three men who were hidden behind a wall. My friend Mary Jo went to sit in the audience, and we had planned for her to give me a hint on which guy I should pick. But when I looked into the audience, she just sat there and didn't move. I didn't know that they had warned the entire crowd against trying to make any signals to the contestants. I passed on an actor and a musician, and picked an accountant, whose suit didn't fit.

We went on a date to the Coconut Grove. A limo picked us up and we had dinner. It was an OK evening, but then the guy started mauling me in the back of the limo. When the driver saw that I was trying to fight the accountant off, he stopped the car, and made the man sit up in the front seat with him!

My second time on The Dating Game, I was one of three women answering questions. A handsome actor named Keir Dullea was the person we were "hoping to date." Keir ended up picking me, but we never went on the date. We were both basically doing the show just to get on TV. We could find our own dates.

The third time I was on the show, was totally unplanned. I had an interview for something else at KTLA, where they taped the show. As I was leaving the interview, Chuck Barris, the creator of the show, and the man who would later host "The Gong Show," came running out into the hallway. He saw me and asked, "Are you married?" I said, "No." He grabbed my arm and said, "Let's go."

As Chuck led me into another studio, he explained that they were ready to tape their special Valentine show, and their celebrity bachelorette Miss America had just gotten engaged and they couldn't use her.

So, by me being in the right place at the right time, I became the Celebrity Valentine Date. Again, I did it just to get on TV, and to also get paid the AFTRA minimum wage for a television appearance. I didn't go on a date with the man I picked, but he was able to take his girlfriend on an all-expenses-paid trip to the Panama Canal.

In 1973, I was in a TV movie called "Blood Sport". When we filmed it, the title was "Poetry in Motion." I had a great scene with Gary Busey, but when the movie came out, they not only changed the name, but they also cut my one and only scene. I still got paid for it though, and even today, when it plays somewhere, I still get residuals, even though my scene ended up on the cutting room floor.

When Gary Busey hit it big with "The Buddy Holly Story," he came to Nashville for the premiere. Hee Haw's Gailard Sartain played "The Big Bopper" in the movie, and even though I wasn't in the movie, Gailard and Gary asked me to attend the red-carpet premiere with them. I still keep in touch with Gary via Facebook.

I had the very unique billing of "Blonde Woman" in the movie "Pretty Boy Floyd," with Martin Sheen. My main job was to lay on a couch and sexily chew on my pearls.

On Sept 26, 1973, I invited my Hee Haw pal, Barbie Benton to a sleepover at my apartment. She had broken up with Hugh Hefner and was dating actor James Stacy. She told me James had planned to take her for a motorcycle ride the next day, and she probably shouldn't spend the night. But I persisted and told her we would have a fun girl's night, making snacks and watching movies.

Barbie agreed to come over and had James drop her off. We enjoyed our sleepover, and the next day, she received a phone call saying that James had been involved in a very serious motorcycle accident. A drunk driver had hit him, and James lost an arm and a leg, and a woman who was riding on the back of James' motorcycle, was killed.

Hugh Hefner knew Barbie had been dating James, and he was out of his mind with worry, thinking she had been killed. But the woman who lost her life was named Claire Cox, but they didn't release her name for a long time.

A decade later, I was in a movie with James Stacy, called "Double Exposure." He hired me for the part, and afterward he told me why, saying "You were the only girl who smiled at me and looked me in the eye, without looking at my missing arm and leg."

1977 saw me in a number of memorable projects. One was a TV movie called "SST Death Flight." There were so many big stars in that movie including, Peter Graves, Bert Convy, Lorne Greene, Regis Philbin, Tina Louise, George Maharis, Robert Reed, and it was the movie debut of Billy Crystal. In one review, a critic said, "It's an all-star cast, but who the hell are Billy Crystal and Misty Rowe?"

In the movie, I played a beauty queen, who was named "Miss SST." I wore a low-cut dress with a bra that pushed my boobs way up and way out. At the end of the film, as the end credits rolled, my name was listed first and was twice as large as everyone else…including Billy Crystal, who was right below me. I know that will never happen again!

During the filming of the movie, Bert Convy flirted with me almost non-stop. He made one comment after another, that today would have gotten him fired. He never once looked me in the eyes, as he leered at my breasts. I was used to crude comments, but he did it so much that it really got irritating. During a break, I finally whispered to him, "I need to go change clothes, but I have something I'd like to give you." Bert smiled, "I'll be in my trailer."

Billy Crystal watched me as I knocked on Bert's door. When he opened it, I took the molded breast cups out of my bra, and said, "Since you like these so much, you can have them!" I threw them at him, and he just howled with laughter. As I stormed off, Billy Crystal gave me a round of applause.

From that moment on, Bert was a totally different man. He was so nice and polite to me. He went on to be one of the all-time great TV game show hosts, and he had Dave Rowland and me on his "Tattletales" show. We played against William Shatner.

Years later, I was playing a saloon showgirl in the pilot for a show called "Young Maverick." I was in the Warner Brothers studio commissary, sitting in the back, when Billy Crystal walked in. By that time, he had become a huge star, and was at the height of his fame. He was sitting at a table with a half dozen high-ups from the studio. But as soon as he glanced over and saw me, he left his group and came over to my table.

Every eye in the cafeteria was on him, as he said, "Hello Misty, how nice to see you again." We had a short visit and I was thrilled and surprised that he even remembered me. I was honored that he took the time to come over to say hello.

I was in the science-fiction TV series "Quark". It was a crazy show about an outer space garbage collector. Buck Henry created the show, and asked me to play an interstellar-communications, alien operator, who had four arms! To get the four-arm effect, they had a girl kneel down behind me, and she stuck her arms out around my body. Her head was right in the middle of my back. You never saw her face on camera, just her arms and hands. They gave us the same manicure, so our hands would match.

Buck Henry was also the main writer on "Saturday Night Live," and he told me that they had a poster of me in my Hee Haw short-shorts on a wall, backstage at SNL.

That same year, I was in an episode of "Kojak" with Telly Savalas. I played a secretary and I had to be a serious, brainy secretary, so I wore glasses. But I don't know if anyone noticed them, as I also wore hot pants, knee-high boots and a tight sweater! Telly Savalas was known for sucking on lollipops and during a break, he gave me one, as he winked and said his catchphrase, "Who loves ya, baby?"

I was in a Bill Murray movie, but unfortunately, it was just before he made it big and it was not a hit at all. It was called "Loose Shoes," but was originally named "Coming Attractions."

In 1979, I did "A Pleasure Doing Business" with Phyllis Diller and Tommy Smothers. I enjoyed working with the legendary Phyllis Diller. Her voice was louder than mine, and she was always fun. My unique billing had me as "The Lucious Prostitute." I guess if you've got to be a prostitute, you might as well be a luscious one! It was one of those absurd parts that seemed to come my way.

But you never know who will happen to see you in something. As silly of a part as that was, it caught the attention of Joyce Selznick, who was a big casting director. And she called me to audition for a role in a new Norman Lear TV series called "Joe's World." Christopher Knight, who was known as Peter Brady on "The Brady Bunch" was the star of the series.

The part I was up for was a woman house painter who breastfed her baby while she was on the job. I wore cut off jeans and a T-shirt that said "Peaches" to my audition. When I got there, they gave me the "sides" to read over as I waited in the hallway, I saw that my character was supposed to be "a tough cookie."

I knew I didn't look very tough in my "Peaches" shirt, so I ran to the lady's room. In a flash, I washed all my makeup off, took off my fake eyelashes and pulled my hair back in a rubber-banded ponytail.

When I went in to read for the part, I did my best to lower my voice and speak as tough and gruff as I possibly could. When I told

Kenny Rogers about this, he laughed and said, "Misty, when you try to talk low and gruff, you end up sounding like a normal woman."

As soon as all the women had auditioned, they told me I had the part. I asked when I would start working, and was shocked when they said, "Right now. Come with us fast." They gave me a script as I walked down the hall. When I opened the door to the studio, I stepped right in the middle of a dress rehearsal for a show that would shoot later that night.

I did quite a few episodes of "Joe's World," but it was only on the air for one year. On Christopher Knight's 21st birthday, during our lunch break, everyone was having the usual sandwiches in the cafeteria. Christopher sadly said, "What a way to celebrate my birthday." I said, "Come on, I'm taking you to lunch." We celebrated his birthday in style at The Spaghetti Factory.

I auditioned for a fairly large role in the movie "The Man with Bogart's Face." It starred Robert Sacchi, who looked exactly like Humphrey Bogart. After going through a few different interviews, I was told they had narrowed their search down to two people...me and Charo. Known for her "Cuchi-Cuchi," and for shaking her large maracas, Charo was a bigger star than I was (in more ways than one) so I wasn't very confident I would get the part. But a few days later, I received a call saying they had chosen me.

I was very excited...until my phone rang again. I had landed the role of Ado Annie in the national tour of "Oklahoma." It was a part I had dreamed of getting. But if I went on the tour, I couldn't do the Bogart movie. I couldn't decide which I should do, so I let my agent Mike Greenfield choose. I turned down "Oklahoma" and reported to the MGM studio to start shooting "The Man with Bogart's Face."

I received very good reviews for my role in the film, with my most memorable scene being with Robert Sacchi, when we had to climb into a trash dumpster. The dumpster, with us in it, was then lifted up and transferred into a garbage truck. We didn't use stuntmen, and Robert and I spent almost four hours down in that hot dumpster.

I got paid very well for the movie, and there was one other perk. At the time, there was a nationwide gas shortage. In Los Angeles, people had to wait in line for hours just to buy a few gallons of gas. But MGM had their own gas station on the studio lot, and I was able to fuel up without waiting in the long lines. I kind of hoped it would take all year for us to complete the movie.

Michelle Phillips was also in "The Man with Bogart's Face." I remembered Michelle from her '60s group the Mamas and the Papas. We both shared the same birthday of June 4th, and we shared the first-class section of a flight to Paris to promote the film at the Cannes Film Festival. The stewardess offered us wine and chocolate. When I told her, I didn't drink, Michelle grabbed my arm and said to the stewardess. "She will have red wine." As the stewardess left, Michelle turned to me and explained, "I will drink my wine and I will drink yours, and you can have both our chocolates." I laughed, "This is the perfect friendship."

Once we landed in Cannes, between Robert's uncanny resemblance to Humphrey Bogart, Michelle's fame from the Mamas and the Papas and my "never met a camera I didn't love" smile, we were mobbed by reporters and paparazzi. I loved every minute of it, but Michelle did not. As the press mobs got bigger, she got more and more frightened, and she finally ran to her hotel room, where she stayed locked inside for most of the trip.

I loved Robert Sacchi. I just adored him, and I worked with him again when I played Lauren Bacall in a touring stage show called "Bogey's Back."

The late '70s and early '80s were busy and exciting times for me. I guest starred in two episodes of "The Love Boat." One of those was a two-part country music themed show. I played Minnie Pearl's niece. Tanya Tucker and my friends from Hee Haw, Lulu Roman and Kenny Price were also on the show.

I usually played Doc Bricker's romantic interest on "Love Boat." I got to know Bernie Kopell very well, as we also worked together in the series "When Things Were Rotten."

People always ask where my "Love Boat" cruise sailed to. The surprising answer is we never left the 20th Century Fox Studio soundstage. We never went on an actual cruise ship. It was all a Hollywood set. "The Love Boat" did occasionally film on location, during real cruises, but not for any of my episodes.

Aaron Spelling was the executive producer of "Love Boat." Aaron's wife Candy had a silver shop in Beverly Hills, and every time I was a guest star on the show, she would send me a beautiful silver vase or picture frame with my name and the date of my episode engraved in the silver.

Over a seven or eight-year period, I really became the darling of Aaron Spelling. It got to where I didn't have to audition for him; he just sent me the scripts.

One day, I came home to one of those scripts for a pilot called "Aloha Paradise." I saw that Debbie Reynolds was going to star in the show, and I also saw that I had only seven lines. Before I finished looking through it, I received a call from the casting director for the show.

When I told him I would probably pass since it wasn't a very big part, he explained, "But it's in Hawaii! You'll get an all-expense paid vacation. You'll be there for 21 days, and you'll only have to work 3 of those. Plus you'll get $175 a day per diem." I laughed, "Well, that's a lot more than the $20 a day I get at "Hee Haw.""

Then he added, "And on top of all that, you'll get paid $10, 000 to say seven lines." Believe it or not, I didn't say 'yes.' Instead, I said, "Let me think it over."

Ten minutes later, the casting director called back. He said, "Mr. Spelling asked for you personally. I just talked to him and he said, "Tell her, she can bring anyone she wants for the three weeks and they'll both fly first class to Hawaii, plus they'll have their own hotel suite and when she's shooting, she'll get her own bungalow on the beach. It was an offer I couldn't turn down.

Guess who I took with me to Hawaii...my favorite boyfriend? A handsome actor? No. I decided to give a little payback to the woman who had given up so much for me over the years. I took my mom, and she had the time of her life. We watched the beautiful Hawaiian sunset every night as we drank Pina Coladas.

On our flight to Hawaii, Mom and I sat in the first class section next to Vicki Lawrence. Vicki was known for her work on "The Carol Burnett Show," and she and her husband had a home in Hawaii. We hit it off instantly and became very close friends.

One year, Vicki helped host a birthday party for me. She was also in a "Love Boat" episode with me. She played Joe Namath's love interest. Vicki was also there for me when my grandpa died. He had lived with me until his death, and the night after he passed, Vicki brought me to her house and cooked me dinner.

That night, in an effort to cheer me up, she played me some highlights of her on "The Carol Burnett Show." The funniest ones featured her dressed as a fat, old woman. She got out her padded, fat suit costume and showed me her wig and glasses. She was only about 30 years old, but she played that old woman character so great, and the more I watched her video clips, the harder I laughed. I told her, "You need to have your own show with this character."

Just a couple years later, she did exactly that, with "Mama's Family."

While the majority of my TV and movie experiences were very positive, there was one that was not. I won't say which movie it was, but it was one of my bigger roles, and before I started filming, I had to get a physical from the studio doctor. Three other girls who were going to be in the movie also had appointments with the same doctor on the same day I did.

A nurse told me to disrobe and put on a little gown. This was the first time I had ever needed to disrobe for a studio physical. The doctor came in and told me to lay down on the table. Then he opened my gown and examined my chest, which I thought was strange. But when he remarked, "I know a lot of women who'd pay good money to have breasts like this," I knew something was very wrong about all of this.

On my way out of the office, the doctor asked me out to lunch! I told him I had a boyfriend and left. The next day, I met the other three actresses in the parking lot, and all of us were strangely quiet. Finally, one asked, "Did anything inappropriate occur during your physical?" Every girl said, 'yes.' One said, "He wanted to give me a pelvic exam!"

We reported him to the assistant director, and he was let go. Things like that are so terrible, especially for young women, and even men, who want to succeed, who want to be "stars" or just want to work and make a living. They shouldn't have to worry about people who will do bad things to them. No one should have to worry about being fired or not being hired if they refuse someone's advances.

In 1982, I appeared in "National Lampoon's Class Reunion" There was another long-haired blonde in the film, and they asked if they could cut my hair, so we would look a little different. As always, I tried to go along with anything that was asked of me, and I let them cut my hair.

Halfway through the movie, my character was killed off. Since we thought my part was done, my agent booked me for a "Love Boat" episode. But at the last minute, the "Class Reunion" director changed the ending of the movie and wanted to include me in the last scene…as a 15-year old. In real life, I was now 32, so I guess I might have been a better actress than many people thought I was!

Greenie, my agent assured the director I would be back in time to film the scene. As soon as I finished on the "Love Boat" set, I took off for the movie location. I ran onto the set, still with all my glamorous makeup and hair, and the director met me, screaming, "Who do you think you are?! You are supposed to be in the campfire scene in ten minutes, and you are supposed to be 15 years old. You sure don't look like a teenager to me!"

I said, "I will be there in ten minutes," as I ran to my dressing room trailer. I washed off every bit of makeup and pulled my hair back into a pigtail. I made it to scene with no time to spare. I was relieved I had pulled it off, but then I learned I had missed another scene that had Chuck Berry playing at a high school dance. The director had planned for me to be the main dancer, but I wasn't there. So, they docked me two day's pay.

I was pretty upset with my agent. As I asked him what happened, he admitted that he just couldn't turn down the money both projects were offering me, so he just overbooked me. But there was no way I could be in two places at once. But having numerous offers was a good thing, and they were starting to pour in.

After "Class Reunion," I came home to find a script on my doorstep. It was for another Aaron Spelling TV show, called "Fantasy Island." From 1980 to 1982, I guest starred in four "Fantasy Island" episodes. I would have done even more, but they did a lot of their filming during the months I was in Nashville, shooting "Hee Haw."

My favorite "Fantasy Island" was one with David Cassidy. In my first scene of the show, I jumped out of a giant cake. I was wearing a tiny, blue bikini.

I did another "Fantasy Island" with George Maharis, and I could tell that he wasn't a very big fan of mine. He didn't like me at all. But I told him that my mom and I used to watch him in "Route 66," and Mom thought he was the most handsome man ever born. At that moment, he totally changed his tune, and was very nice to me for the rest of our shoot.

Ricardo Montalban, who starred as Mr. Roarke, directed the last episode I was in. Afterward, I received two dozen red roses from Arthur Rowe, who was the producer of the episode. He also included a note, saying what a great job I had done. I was so thrilled, especially since after ten years on Hee Haw, the only gift I had received was a "Hee Haw" cap!

On my last day shooting "Fantasy Island," I made a homemade cake and brought it for everyone on the set. I also got to spend some time with Ricardo Montalban when we were both guest celebrities at the Indianapolis 500. Merv Griffin was also there, and they let us both be in the pace car as it drove around the famous racetrack.

Ricardo brought his very handsome son along. He and I were about the same age, and we really hit it off. Once the race started, the special guests had a suite way up in a tower over the finish line, and Ricardo's son and I spent most of the day together.

At lunchtime, we decided to go downstairs and get a couple hot dogs. When we came back up, Ricardo's son went to the restroom and Ricardo walked over to me and whispered, "You know Misty, my son is engaged to be married." I said, "Oh, yes, he told me. We were just getting hotdogs." And in his wonderful Latin accent, Ricardo joked, "Well, when you are looking for hotdogs, be sure you don't find the wienie."

As I write this, I guess we should move on from hotdogs and wienies to…meatballs.

I played the crazy part of Fanny Bentwood (where do they come up with those names?!) in the motion picture "Meatballs Part 2." Fanny Bentwood was the girl's camp counselor that all the teenage boys were in love with. Paul Reubens, who was known as Pee Wee Herman played the camp bus driver. We had a lot of scenes together.

When I was first cast for the movie, its name was "Call Me Meathead," and I thought Rob Reiner (Meathead in "All In The Family") was going to be in it. As I walked onto the set, Rob Reiner was nowhere to be found, but Cinnamon the bear was. Cinnamon was a trained bear that chased us throughout the movie.

When the bear wasn't in a scene, they always secured him with a steel neck collar and chain. But Cinnamon was so well-trained that when he did a scene and the director yelled, "Cut!", he'd walk directly over to his chain and collar and put it on his neck all by himself. Cinnamon loved chocolate milk, and when he wasn't on set, he was usually drinking chocolate milk out of a baby bottle.

In 1985, I did a memorable episode of "Silver Spoons" with Ricky Schroder and the great John Houseman. The episode was titled "The Trouble with Grandfather," and I was the trouble. In the show, John Houseman had fallen for a young, sexy cowgirl. When I went to my audition, I tried to channel Grand Ole Opry star Dottie West. She always dressed and acted so sexy, so I dressed in a tight, all-white western outfit, complete with a cowboy hat. The moment I walked in to read for the part, I was the loudest, over-the-top, country girl you've ever seen. The casting directors had no idea what hit them, and when I finally stopped talking and singing, they simply said, "There's our girl."

When I guest-starred on an episode of "Matt Houston," Sid Caesar and Jimmy Coco were also on the same show. I had met Sid on the series "When Things Were Rotten," but he rarely said anything to me between takes. But on the "Matt Houston" show, he seemed like a totally different person. He took me to a nearby deli, and he insisted on walking me to my car when we worked into the evening.

I finally told him, "Sid, you are so wonderful. But the first time we worked together, you wouldn't talk to me at all." Sid, very honestly admitted, "I was drunk back then. I had a terrible drinking habit. My wife said she was going to leave me if I kept drinking, so I just quit. And I am a better man today." He definitely was.

In 1985, I enjoyed the greatest roll of my career on television. I played a country singer on "Airwolf." When I first read for the part, the director told me, "Your stage presence is wonderful, but I think you might be too pretty for this." I said, "Let me come back tomorrow." He did, and I walked in, wearing jeans with a rope for my belt. I had no makeup on and I hadn't touched my hair since I got out of bed.

The director laughed and said, "OK, maybe you are not pretty all the time." But then he added, "We've promised our favorite booking agent that we'd audition her client." I asked who and was immediately dejected when he said, "It's Barbie Benton." I tried to be upbeat (but failed) when I said, "Well, thank you for giving me your time."

I went to my car, knowing Barbie would get the part. After all, she was a real country singer, with a major record deal. But as I opened my car door, I looked in the backseat and saw my newly released, and quickly best-selling poster. The poster company had just given me 100 of them to give to my friends.

I grabbed one of the rolled-up posters and ran back up to the director's office. The receptionist asked, "Did you forget something?" I said, "I sure did," as I barged right into the director's closed door. I said, "I know Barbie has records, but I have this..." I unrolled the 2 x 3 foot poster, put it on his desk and walked right out. When the director looked at me and my life-sized short-shorts, Barbie didn't have a chance. Sorry Barbie!

I played the role of "Roxy" and worked with the stars of the series Jan-Michael Vincent and the legendary Ernest Borgnine. Ernest was close friends with George "Goober" Lindsey, and had visited the "Hee Haw" set many times.

I had so many lines in the show, that I spent most of my breaks reading my script. Ernest Borgnine came over and asked what I was doing and when I said I was memorizing my lines, he sat down, grabbed my script and said, "I'll run them with you."

Jan-Michael Vincent was known as "the bad boy of the lot." But he was just gorgeous, and he couldn't have been nicer to me. He volunteered to feed me lines for all my close-up, reaction shots. A lot of stars make someone else do that while they go to their dressing room trailer. But Jan-Michael stayed on the set, even though he wasn't on camera, because he knew his effort would help make me more believable. I will never forget his kindness.

I had to do all my own singing and dancing, and they built a huge stage just for me on the Universal lot. It was just across a little meadow from the Bates Motel from the movie "Psycho", and I liked to sit on the steps of the Bates Motel as I ate my box lunch.

We shot our scenes with the Airwolf helicopter off the lot, in the Agoura Hills. They gave me a helmet that weighed about 40 pounds. I could barely hold my head up when I wore it.

A short time after the show aired, I ran into Noel Blanc, the man who had gotten me my first agent 15 years earlier. Noel said, "Misty, I always wondered what happened to that sweet young girl I met. I hoped she didn't get taken advantage of. Then I saw you were working for Mel Brooks, and I thought, Misty's fine." Then Noel added, "I just saw you on "Airwolf," and you were so great, you should have been nominated for an Emmy."

Noel told me that if I didn't get an Emmy, then maybe I should at least get involved with the Emmys. He helped me become a blue-ribbon judge for the Emmys. I nominated actors and actresses for comedies. I loved doing that for a couple years, and I was also on the nominee committee for the Screen Actors Guild Awards.

After stepping off the "Airwolf" helicopter, I got on a plane to head to Taipei for one of my most interesting films. It was called "Mob Busters" and was about an American who was fighting the mob in Hong Kong. I got top billing, along with Richard Kiel, the 7-foot, 2-inch man who played "Jaws" in the James Bond movies.

When we arrived in Taipei, we found that none of the crew spoke English. As I stepped off the plane, the movie director, producer and a Chinese leading man all bowed down to me. I smiled at Richard and said, "I think I'm going to like it here." But they warned me that when I wasn't filming, I should stay in my hotel, because they were quite concerned I would be kidnapped. An interpreter explained, "No one here looks like you. They are fascinated by your long blonde hair." I found out how fascinated they were, when they started calling me "Princess Golden Hair."

When we filmed on a boat dock, in between scenes, when I brushed my hair, the moment I put my brush down, someone came and picked all the hair strands out of the brush. I asked why they did that, and they replied, "Mee-chee," (their pronunciation of "Misty") "Mee-chee hair is golden root." They had never seen hair color like mine.

They had also never seen someone as tall as Richard Kiel. Every store owner and local resident came running out to catch a glimpse of the gentle giant. They snapped pictures, pointed and giggled at him, but he took it all in stride, a giant stride that he was used to by then. Richard's wife was with him, and the locals were also curious how a man over 7 feet tall could be married to a woman who was shorter than I was. They asked, "How do they fit?" I didn't even try to answer that one.

I got paid a lot of money to do the movie, but I had my agent put it in my contract that I would absolutely do no nudity. I told them I wasn't going to take off anything. I kept my word and kept my clothes on. But when the movie poster came out, it had a huge drawing of me nude, as I held some envelopes over my private parts. I thought, "How do I get myself into these things?"

Eddie Liu, the leading man, who lived in Taiwan, asked if I would go sightseeing with him, and he took me to the "Land of a Thousand Buddhas." Then he took me to meet his family. Over dinner, he interpreted for his parents who spoke no English. His mother's first question to me was, "Do you have AIDS?" When I said, "No! No, I don't have AIDS," she asked, "Do you have the herpes?" I laughed and answered, "No, I don't have herpes."

With those initial inquiries out of the way, his mom brought out a box with a beautiful coral necklace. She presented it to me, and I put it around my neck. As Eddie drove me back to my hotel, he quietly announced, "Now we are engaged." I asked, "What?" He explained that their custom says when a mother gives a gift to a woman and she puts it on, it shows she has accepted her son to be her husband.

But the marriage never happened. Eddie couldn't get a visa to the U.S. But I was surprised a couple years later, when his mother and aunt showed up at my Los Angeles home. We took photos and had a nice visit, but I never returned to Taiwan.

As I look back on my resume, I have to admit that I have done quite a few strange films. I also did more than a dozen TV pilots for series, including one with "Batman's" Adam West called "The Last Precinct." In 1991, I was also in an episode of "MacGiver." That turned out to be my last prime time TV appearance, before I moved east to support my husband's career and raise our daughter.

I loved being a working actress. "Working" is the key word in that sentence. For all actors and actresses, there are many times when you don't work. During those down times, most actors have to find a "day job." But from the time I was 20 years old, any job I had was show-business related. I was either acting, singing, dancing or directing.

I may not have been a huge star, but I did shine from time to time. They say that only 5% of the Screen Actors Guild makes a living from acting. Only 5% of all actors can sustain themselves throughout their lifetime. So, I consider myself to be very blessed.

MY BEST FRIEND MARRIES A GAMBLER

I became close, life-long friends with many of my Hee Haw cast members. But my very-best friend on the show was Marianne Gordon. She would later become Marianne Rogers when she married country star Kenny Rogers.

Marianne and I started working on Hee Haw on the same day. The show been on the air for three years, before Marianne and I were added to the cast. Another girl, Anne Randell was also hired at the same time. Anne didn't stay on the show very long, but Marianne and I would spend the next two decades there.

Since we were the "new girls" coming into an established cast, Marianne and I stuck together, similar to new kids entering a strange, new school.

When I started on Hee Haw, I had $20 in my pocket, and no credit cards. The show producers told me each cast member would get a per diem of $25 each day to cover their food and other expenses while we were in Nashville. I knew I could make my $20 last until I got my per diem. Then I found out they didn't actually give you the per diem money until the end of the week, so I was totally broke by the middle of my first week.

A bunch of the other girls in the cast were going to lunch and they asked me to come along. I said, "I would love to, but I don't have any money. Could someone lend me $5?" There was an instant chill in the room. Everyone looked away or down at the floor.

After a moment, Marianne Gordon reached into her purse and pulled out a $20 bill. She didn't just loan me five, she loaned me twenty. It was also the first of many, many times that Marianne would show her love, kindness and generosity to me. Years later, I reminded her of that day, and she said, "When I handed you that twenty, I thought, 'This girl is such a ditz, I will never see this money again.'

Marianne and I were part of one of Hee Haw's most popular and longest running sketches. It also featured Gunilla Hutton and Lulu Roman, and we were all called the 'Gossipy Girls.' We opened each sketch by singing, "Now, we're not ones to go 'round spreadin' rumors..." Lulu, Marianne and Gunilla were also very good singers, but I was not. In our first tapings, I sang as quietly as I could, in hopes the others girl's voices would cover mine up.

After a few takes, the producer, Sam Lovullo walked over and said, "Girls, this sketch is just not funny if you all sing perfectly. Misty, do you think you could sing a little off key?" I coyly responded, "Well, I could try." As I grew more and more comfortable on camera and with the sketch, my very off-key voice got louder and louder, and eventually overpowered and almost covered up the other three girls.

Marianne usually had to stand next to me, and once we became very good friends, she admitted, "Misty Rowe, your voice is so high and so screechy and so loud. On days when we had to do that skit over and over, when I go home at night, my ears are still ringing." From our second year on, Marianne stuffed her ears with cotton balls anytime she had to stand next to me while I sang!

By the way, back to the lyrics of that song… "We're really not the gossipy kind." I had thought about naming this book, "I really AM the gossipy kind!"

The direction of Marianne's life changed when a guest star came to Hee Haw in 1975. The guest was pretty husky, with long hair, an earring and pink glasses. I remember thinking he looked like a big lion wearing pink glasses. When he walked onto the set, I was sitting next to a musician and I asked, "Who is that?" They answered, "That's Kenny Rogers. He used to be somebody."

Kenny's group, The First Edition, had broken up and he was now on his own. At the time, he was singing in bars and lounges. But just three years later, not only would Kenny Rogers be a "somebody" again, he would be one of country music's biggest stars. He would also be married to Marianne Gordon.

Marianne's life with Kenny started out very normal. They lived in an apartment, where they'd invite me over. Marianne cooked dinner and Kenny made us a cake out of a box. Then they moved to a little house. Marianne used to cut and style Kenny's hair and trim his beard. They just adored each other, and they were so sweet and adorable together.

In late 1976, Kenny recorded the song "Lucille", and Kenny and Marianne's life was never the same again. "Lucille" became one of the biggest hits of all-time, and it propelled Kenny to super stardom. A year after "Lucille", he hit the jackpot again with "The Gambler."

One day as I was visiting with Marianne and Kenny, as he looked around their huge mansion, Kenny told me, "Having money is great, and it certainly can make your life more comfortable. But money cannot make you happy." He continued, "People see my success and they think being rich and famous must be the greatest thing in the world. But I've found that it's really not about the destination. It's about the journey. It's not about where you end up; it's about the steps you take along the way, and the people you meet on your journey."

As I look back at my own journey in this book, I realize I've met so many wonderful people along the way. I have so many people to thank for helping me along my way.

Marianne Gordon Rogers probably knows me better than anybody else. She has been the most gracious, loving, kind and generous person I have ever met in my life. From 1972 to 2013, Marianne was such a big part of my life. Today, even though we don't live in the same state, and I sometimes don't see her in person for years, I know that I can call her, and she will be there for me.

Marianne and Kenny were there for me during the darkest moment of my life. I had just broken up with my boyfriend David and I was heartbroken. At my lowest point, I tried to take my own life.

A short time later, I was with Marianne and she saw cuts on my wrists. I told her I had scratched myself in my rose bushes. When she told Kenny about it, he immediately knew what had really happened. From that moment, they both put their arms around me spiritually. They asked me to go to church with them, and they'd invite me to dinner, to the movies, or to go shopping. Marianne and I enjoyed going on long walks and of course we attended lots of Kenny's concerts.

Kenny was playing huge, sold out arenas and just before the lights went down, a security guard would bring Marianne and me out to sit in the front row. When Dolly Parton opened for Kenny, we would spend time visiting with her backstage. I also went with them to an awards show at the Grand Ole Opry house.

We were backstage and Marianne introduced me to a friend of hers. His name was Dave Rowland and he was having some big country hits with his group "Dave and Sugar." Dave and I immediately hit it off and we began seeing each other. I dated Dave for the next four years.

People always ask if I dated anyone from Hee Haw. I never did. No, Junior and I were not romantically involved! Dave Rowland was also the only country music artist I dated. I probably would have married him, but he was always on the road, living on his tour bus, and that was just not the life for me.

Before he made it big in country music, Dave was part of the Stamps Quartet that sang backup for Elvis Presley. Elvis had given him numerous pieces of jewelry, and Dave even got a car from Elvis. Dave was so proud of that car, and I knew he really loved me when he let me drive it!

I was driving that car, heading to film Hee Haw early one morning. About halfway there, I was broadsided by another car. They hit me in the passenger side. My windshield exploded and the top of my car ripped off. I heard my bones snapping. It reminded me of China cups and plates breaking. I knew I was hurt very badly. By the time the paramedics arrived, I had passed out.

I had broken six ribs and one was broken in two places, and it had gone into my lung. I also had a concussion. I was hospitalized for 10 days. When I came to, my first thought was, 'How am I going to tell Dave that I destroyed his Elvis car?' I knew he was going to hate me. But Dave showed his love for me, and his sense of humor, when he went to the junkyard to see his wrecked car. He brought me a picture he had taken in front of the car and he was holding a sign that said, "Call BR-549."

Besides all the pain I was in, I also felt bad because I was going to miss the entire two weeks of Hee Haw tapings. But one of my first visitors in the hospital was Sam Lovullo, and he brought me a check for the same amount that I would have made for that season.

Kenny and Marianne Rogers also came to see me. Their visit turned into quite a circus. Kenny was at the height of his fame, and as he walked through the lobby, he was mobbed by fans. When she came into my room, Marianne said, "Kenny will be here shortly. When I left him, he was signing an autograph for a patient whose backside was showing through their hospital gown."

A few weeks later, after I was mending at home, Sam asked if I felt good enough to come film some "Wild lines." Those are very short takes of just one person saying something like, "Here's Buck," "That joke was corny," or "We'll be right back after this."

When I got to the studio, it was just me, Sam and a camera man. Sam explained, "If you can just sit in a chair and read these cue cards, we'll insert you into the show and no one at home will ever know anything."

I couldn't move one arm and they filmed me from the shoulders up, but Sam was right. No one ever knew I had just gotten out of the hospital. I ended up in every single show that season, and not only did I get paid for the season, but I still get residuals from those shows.

When Kenny Rogers started having one hit after another, especially with The Gambler and Lucille, and once Marianne and Kenny had a child, she thought she should probably give up her Hee Haw job. Of course, she didn't need the money, but she did enjoy being on the show. When Sam agreed that she could do all her tapings in just one day, every six months, she agreed to stay on.

In 1981, we had a severe windstorm in California. Of course, my home that was built in 1928 had very old windows, and almost every one was blown out. I had to get a loan for $11, 000 to replace them. At that same time, my mother's car broke down. To fix it would have cost more than her old car was worth. I wanted to help her, but I had no money at all.

Marianne and Kenny had a home in Beverly Hills and when they found out about my mom's car, Marianne told me, "I just talked to Kenny. We love your family so much and we are so blessed with everything that's happened with Kenny's career. And we would like you to do us the honor of letting us buy your mother a car." I couldn't believe it. Marianne instructed me to not tell my mom because they wanted to surprise her.

Marianne invited mom and me to a luncheon at her home. Former Miss America, Phyllis George was also there. After lunch, we went outside, and Marianne had mom's car waiting in the driveway. I said, "Mama, they got a car for you," and she put her head down on the hood and just cried and cried. Mom loved that car so much.

Marianne's kindness to my mother continued for the rest of my mom's life. When she went into a nursing facility with Alzheimer's, every month she would receive a card or a gift of flowers or candy from Marianne. The nurses who cared for Mom couldn't believe how those cards and flowers continued to come from Marianne.

Kenny and Marianne were also so generous to me when I got married. They paid for my wedding reception, and it was no small affair. That would have been much more than enough, but Kenny said he wanted to give me another gift. He was an amazingly talented photographer, and he asked if he could take my wedding portrait. In the picture section of this book, you can see the wonderful photo of me in my wedding dress that Kenny Rogers took.

I once did a photo shoot with the famous photographer Harry Langdon. The photos made me look so much more glamorous than I really was. I told Kenny I couldn't believe how amazing the photos were. Kenny said, "I can do the same thing Harry does. It's all about the lighting and I learned lighting straight from Harry."

Kenny became such a great photographer, that he took portraits of numerous celebrities, ranging from Michael Jackson to President Ronald Reagan. But for a number of years, I was one of his favorite models. He took hundreds of photos of me, and he gave them all to me at no charge.

In December of 1992, I awoke one morning with a feeling that I should call Marianne. I dialed her and as soon as she picked up, she confided, "Kenny and I are getting a divorce." I was shocked and heartbroken for both of them.

Kenny and Marianne were dear friends. Marianne is still so important in my life. But when they divorced, my relationship with Kenny ended, and I never saw him again. On March 20, 2020, when I heard that Kenny had died, I immediately called Marianne. I didn't think she would answer, but she did. We talked about 45 minutes, as we reminisced about all the wonderful times we all had together.

THE ONES THAT GOT AWAY

I am so thankful for each and every acting role I've had in my career. I'm grateful for all of them…including the very small ones, and even those in movies that turned out to be "bombs!" Hey, maybe that makes me a blonde bombshell!

But for every part I landed, there were many others that I didn't get. I sometimes wonder how my life would have turned out if I had gotten hired for some of those. Here are a few of "the ones that got away."

In 1972, I got called to audition for a movie called "American Graffiti." My character had no words in the script, and it was a very small part. I was going to just be driving around in a white Thunderbird. After two call backs, they said I was a little young for the part, and the role went to Suzanne Somers. One of the main stars of the movie was Ron Howard. Even though I missed out on "American Graffiti," less than two years later, I would get the chance to work with Ron when I was hired to play Wendy the Car-Hop on "Happy Days!"

During one of my "Happy Days" episodes, Cheryl Ladd guest-starred as a movie star who Richie won a date with. A few years later, Cheryl became a superstar when she replaced Farrah Fawcett on Charlie's Angels. Cheryl stayed on the show for four years, and when she left in 1981, guess who almost became a Charlie's Angel...yep, me. But my mother blew it for me!

My agent, Mike Greenfield got me the audition, and I drove my 1936 Cord Roadster to the 20th Century Fox studios. I loved that car, but it always had problems, and on my way to the interview, my car broke down. My mom was living in Redlands at the time and she came and picked me up and took me to the audition.

She waited in the car as I went inside a little bungalow where the casting director and producer were waiting. They gave me my script and I started learning my lines. It was a very hot day and they had all of the windows to the bungalow open. You could hear the birds and traffic outside.

Just as I started my audition, I heard my mother screaming in the parking lot! She was giving directions to someone who was trying to back a big truck in, and her voice was much higher pitched and screeching than mine ever was. As I tried to keep doing my lines, my mom continued to yell, very loudly. The producer stopped me and asked, "Who is that terrible woman out there and why is she screaming with that horrible voice?" They ran over and closed the windows. Then the casting director asked, "Misty, do you know that woman?" I said, "I have no idea." I immediately felt like St. Peter! I had denied my own mother.

It all threw me off so much that I blew the entire audition. When I got to the car, my mom asked how I did. I told her, "I don't think I will ever be an angel."

Can you imagine the Superman movies with Misty Rowe as Eve Teschmacher instead of Valerie Perrine? It almost happened!

I was at a dinner party, where I met an older agent named Kurt Frings. I had always wanted to meet him because he had been Marilyn Monroe's agent. He was also an agent for Audrey Hepburn, Marlon Brando and Elizabeth Taylor. I was very honored when Kurt said he would like to be my agent.

One of the first bigtime auditions he got for me was for the Superman movie. Kurt had already gotten Marlon Brando a cameo in the movie and when he told me he was getting paid three million dollars, I knew that I was about to win the lottery!

Luckily, I didn't spend any of that money, because I didn't get the part. The producers wanted to see more film on me and when they found my "Goodbye Norma Jean" movie, they quickly backed out. Kurt called me and yelled, "That movie was Kryptonite to Superman! Don't you ever do another piece of crap like that again. You can't be a big star if you do those low budget things. You almost got the part, but then they saw that terrible movie." He really let me have it.

Having a major role in Superman would have been great. But having a lead in Smokey would have been even better. In 1977, I was up for the role as Burt Reynolds' love interest in "Smokey and the Bandit."

Hal Needham was Burt Reynolds' best friend. Hal wrote the screenplay for "Smokey and the Bandit." I auditioned for the movie and then they called me to come back for a second reading. My confidence grew when they called me a third time. When I went in, Hal Needham's assistant whispered to me, "I want you to know that you are Hal's first choice. We want you to do exactly what you did at your callback. Do not change anything."

I knew I had never been so close to the "big time." All of my years of acting study and work had come to this. This is where I had to show what I could do. And...I nailed it. My screen test was perfect. Everyone was thrilled.

A few days later, my agent called. He said, "You did such a great job Misty, and I am so sorry." He explained that when Hal Needham went to show Burt Reynolds my "perfect" screen test, Burt told him, "Hal, I went to a party last night and met Sally Field. I don't want to see any screen tests. I want Sally."

If I had gotten that part, it would have changed a lot of things. Of course, it would have changed my life, but it would have also changed Burt and Sally's lives. But I thought she was so good in the film, and of course they had such amazing chemistry and you could see them falling in love as the movie went on.

I did land a role in a Norman Lear TV series called "Joe's World." Norman Lear liked me so much that he asked me to audition for his spinoff of "All in the Family". Carroll O'Connor was going to star in "Archie's Place." In the show, Archie owned a bar and they were looking for someone to play his main waitress.

My agent, Mike Greenfield, told me I should use my "tough, New Jersey accent." He also told me I would be paid $10, 000 just to do the pilot for the show. I was overjoyed. I was going to get to work with a TV legend, who was playing his classic character Archie Bunker, and I was going to get paid a huge amount of money. It sounded almost too good to be true!

But once again, at the very last moment, everything fell through. My first clue that something was wrong came when the studio didn't deliver my script to me. Then they didn't call to tell me what time I should be at the studio. A short time later, my agent called with the bad news.

He explained that when they told Carroll O' Connor they had found a beautiful, funny girl to play the part of his waitress, he said,

"Beautiful girls are not funny. Get me a gay guy to be a waiter. Gay guys are funny."

So, I didn't get that part. But there was some good news. I still got my $10, 000. Since they had hired me with an AFTRA contract, they had to follow through on our financial agreement.

In the late 1970s and early '80s, one of the most popular shows on television was the ABC sit-com "Three's Company." John Ritter, Joyce Dewitt and Suzanne Somers were the stars of the show. But when Suzanne Somers left "Three's Company," every girl in Hollywood wanted to be her replacement. Every girl…including me. I tried out for the spot, but the job was given to Jenilee Harrison.

But I did get to know John Ritter quite well. He was in my acting class at Stella Adler's Workshop. John had a great sense of humor and was fun to be around. One day in Stella's class, John watched as I did a scene from "The Goddess." When I had finished, he loudly said, "I'd like to see Suzanne Somers do that!" It made me feel very good.

BROADWAY...JOE

Every stage actress dreams of making it big on Broadway. In 1980, I spent a couple months on stage with Broadway...Broadway Joe Namath.

I had never done a big musical before, so I was quite surprised when my agent Mike Greenfield called me and said, "I've got you an audition for the national tour of 'Li'l Abner.' They are looking for Daisy Mae, and I can't think of anyone more perfect than a Hee Haw girl." Greenie continued, "If you get it, your leading man will be Joe Namath." Of course, Joe Namath was a football legend, and when his NFL career ended, he went into acting.

When I got that call, I was with my boyfriend, Dave Rowland. Dave had made it big with his country group Dave and Sugar and he was opening for Kenny Rogers. As soon as we found out I would be required to do some serious singing for 'Li'l Abner,' Dave took me to meet with Kenny Rogers' musical director, Edgar Struble. Edgar and Dave then set out to give me a crash course in singing. When they weren't working on Kenny's show, they were helping me learn my songs.

I flew to Los Angeles to audition at the Dorothy Chandler Pavilion. I was quite nervous because this really was a big deal. The chance to be the lead in a national tour production like this doesn't come along every day. But thanks to the hard work and effort of Dave Rowland and Edgar Struble, I nailed my audition!

A short time later, I went to meet Joe Namath. Oh, did I tell you that I knew almost nothing about football? But my older brother Ed sure did. When he found out I was going to work with Joe, he couldn't believe it. He said, "Joe is one of the greatest of all time!"

I was nervous about meeting Joe. I knew I would revert to my shy self. But when I walked in the room, I was shocked to see that Joe was wearing a T-shirt with my picture on it! He stuck out his hand and said, "Hi, I'm Joe." Seeing my photo on his chest instantly put me at ease, and also showed me that he had a great sense of humor.

Our first rehearsals were at the Peachtree Plaza Theater of the Stars in Atlanta. Two dozen young singers and dancers and a 20-piece orchestra were also learning their parts. Yes, this was a big production.

Stockton Briggle was our director as we did the musical almost every night, for two months. But there was one night that I will never forget. It took place at the St. Louis Municipal Opera. When I first saw the 11, 000 seat, outdoor Muny, I couldn't believe my eyes. The entire amphitheater was so beautiful, and it seemed that the seats went back as far as I could see...and for our show, every seat was sold!

The night before our St. Louis show, we had played in Atlanta. Since our crew had to come straight from Georgia, the costume department didn't have time to get my Daisy Mae outfit dry-cleaned. Instead, they took my polka dotted bustier and dipped it into a strong dry-cleaning fluid. It was kind of like formaldehyde. I had no idea they had done that, but it was no big deal. What could go wrong?

In the middle of our performance, as I sang and danced, I started to perspire. And when my sweat started mixing with that dry-cleaning fluid, my chest started to burn. I really thought I was on fire, and when I looked down, I saw these huge red welts popping up in my cleavage.

At intermission, I ran off stage and ripped my top off. I started splashing myself with water as I yelled, "It's burning me! It's burning me!" The next day, a newspaper reviewer wrote, "It was spontaneous combustion for the alluring Misty Rowe, who set the stage on fire."

It seemed there was never a dull moment during my tour with Joe Namath. One night, during an outdoor show, it started to rain, and it was just pouring. Our 20-piece orchestra got up and ran for cover. They didn't want to get their brass instruments ruined. But the audience stayed where they were. They just got out their umbrellas and stayed in their seats.

When Joe and I saw that, we decided to stay out on stage. Joe looked at me and laughed, "You know any songs?" I wiped the water out of my eyes and said, "What about 'Singing in the Rain?'", and we gave them a very impromptu version, since neither one of us had ever sung it before.

One day, when I came in for a rehearsal, I saw that Joe was wearing a baseball cap that he had pulled way down. I gave him my usual big smile and asked, "Hey, Joe, how are you today?"

But instead of his usual happy greeting, I heard, "My hair is green." I asked, "What?" Joe took his cap off and his hair was bright green.

He had wanted to turn his brown hair black so it would match the Li'l Abner cartoon. But instead of black hair, his turned green. They had to fly in a hairstylist from New York, and after going through a multi-hour process, they managed to get him back to his original hair color by showtime.

Joe was not a great singer. Of course, neither was I, but he was a great celebrity. He was a great star, and when he walked out on stage, there was a loud roar from the audience like I had never heard before. He attracted huge crowds and so much publicity for our production. People magazine came out and did a big piece on our musical. It ran with a full-page picture of me and Joe together. Newsweek magazine also ran a photo of us. It was really amazing.

My friend Marianne Gordon Rogers came to see us at a performance, and we planned to go out to dinner with Joe afterward. We all got in a limo that was in an underground parking area. But the moment our car came out of the parking lot, we were instantly surrounded by a crowd of a couple thousand people. They just swarmed our car. The driver couldn't go forward and couldn't back up.

Joe opened the sunroof and stood up, so his head and shoulders were above the roof of the car. He looked at all of those fans who were trying to get to him and he calmly said, "Thank you all for coming tonight. We had such a great time performing for you. I'd love to sign autographs, but my Daisy Mae needs to get some dinner. You can take my picture for a minute or so here, but then we'll need to head on."

After smiling for photos, Joe came back down in the car, and his crowd of fans all stepped out of the way so our car could get through. As we started to roll, I exclaimed, "This is like the parting of the Red Sea!" But Joe had that kind of power. Men loved him. Many had grown up watching him play football and he was their hero. Of course, women loved him. Joe had quite a reputation as a lady's man, and even though he was an amazing quarterback, he never made a pass at me. I kind of wondered why, but one day he informed me, "I was once told that I should never come on to my leading lady." So, we never dated. He gave me a friendly kiss or two, but we never dated.

During the show, there was a scene where Joe was supposed to drink a secret love potion from a big bottle. Each night, by the time the scene came around, Joe was usually thirsty, so they always filled up the bottle with water and he chugged it down as quickly as he could.

But on closing night, before the show, I filled Joe's prop bottle with moonshine. It was the real thing and it was strong alcohol. When the moment came for him to take a drink, I watched as he took the biggest gulp he possibly could. As soon as it hit the back of his throat, he yelled, "Daisy!" I took off running and he chased me around the stage until he finally caught me. And I can honestly say that I was tackled by Joe Namath. The crowd just went crazy.

Working with Joe Namath on our national tour was one of the true highlights of my life. I just adored him.

A few years after our tour, I went to see Joe as he performed in the musical "Sugar" at the Dorothy Chandler Pavilion. Before the show, I asked a worker to take a note backstage to Joe to tell him I was in the audience. As the show went on, I doubted whether he ever saw my note. Once the musical was over, as the audience started filing out, a man came over to me and said, "Miss Rowe, Joe would like to see you and your date backstage." Joe introduced us to his fiancé, and he was still just as nice as he was when we were touring together.

But Joe wasn't the only famous NFL player I worked with. I appeared in "Damn Yankees" with Dallas Cowboy Harvey Martin. He had been the Most Valuable Player of Super Bowl XII.

I got that job through a chain of events that began when I attended a party, where I met Johnny Crawford. Johnny had been a child-star when he was one of the original Mickey Mouse Mouseketeers, and he was also in "The Rifleman," with Chuck Connors. Johnny suggested that I try to join up with his equity agent Joan Kovats.

I met with Joan and she already had a part lined up for me. It was for the role of Lola, the sexiest woman on earth in "Damn Yankees." Harvey Martin was going to play the devil, and our debut would be at Granny's Dinner Playhouse, which was the largest dinner theater in the country.

"Granny's" was in Dallas, Texas and bunch of Harvey's Dallas Cowboy teammates came to see our production. My big moment in the musical came when I sang "Whatever Lola Wants, Lola Gets." During that song, I was supposed to take off a frilly piece of my sexy wardrobe and toss is across the stage. But when I saw all those Dallas Cowboys in the front rows, I got so excited that I really gave it a huge throw. The clothing sailed over Shoeless Joe's head and landed right on a hook on the wall. I couldn't have done it again in a million tries. The audience, and all of those football players just exploded in applause. The next day's newspaper review was the best one I ever received, mainly because of that clothing toss I made. Harvey and I did "Damn Yankees" at Granny's every night, for almost a month.

Minnesota Vikings' quarterback Fran Tarkenton made a lot of great throws in his career. I once told him one of my Hee Haw "Bedtime Stories." I had written one especially for him, and I performed it during a fundraising event.

For someone who knew very little about sports, I probably worked with more sports stars than just about anyone. And if things had worked out differently, I might have married one of those.

Terry Bradshaw is another NFL legend. He was one of the greatest quarterbacks ever. But I met him on the golf course. Terry was playing in one of George "Goober" Lindsey's golf tournaments. Each year, George brought in lots of different stars to raise money for charity. I was a celebrity hostess of the event, and I handed out prizes and signed autographs. That's what I was doing when Terry Bradshaw saw me.

At the time, I really didn't know who Terry was. But I was about to find out! After the event, we both happened to be on the same plane, flying to Los Angeles. When Terry saw that I had an empty seat next to me, he asked if he could sit down. We visited during the flight and when we landed, he asked for my number.

A week later, my phone rang. When I said "Hello", I heard, "Misty, this is Terry Bradshaw, and I want to know if you want to marry me." I was so shocked, and stammered, "We've never even been out on a date. I couldn't possibly marry someone I don't know."

Terry said, "Well, I'm not asking you to get married to me. I'm asking if you want to marry me, because I'm a good Christian and I cannot waste my time dating a woman who does not want to marry me."

I couldn't tell if he was joking or serious, but he kept calling once a week and each time, he would ask, "Do you want to marry me?" But one day the calls stopped, and Terry married someone else. He was quite a character.

STAGE 4…AND MICHAEL JACKSON IS OPERATING

We never know what is coming our way. One night, I went to bed after bringing down the house with my performance in "Damn Yankees" in Dallas. When I woke up the next morning, I couldn't swallow. I was also very tired. I managed to get out of bed a little after noon, but I was just dragging.

As soon as I got back home to Los Angeles, I went to the throat specialist. After checking me over, he said, "I don't think your throat is your problem. I think something is wrong with your thyroid."

An examination by a thyroid doctor showed that I had seven suspicious lumps in my neck. The doctor said they would have to do a needle biopsy in each one, once a month as they gave me treatment. A couple months into that, after one biopsy, I received a call from the doctor. He asked me to come back in so he could talk to me. I thought, "Well, that is never good news." I was right. As soon as I got to the doctor's office, he said, "You have stage 4 cancer."

I was stunned. I was also all alone. I had no husband, no boyfriend, no kids. As I drove home by myself, my thoughts went back to everything the doctor had just told me. I know I had zoned out during a lot of it, but I did remember him saying they would do surgery to try to remove it, and I would also need chemotherapy.

The first thing I did when I got home was to call my lawyer to have him draw up a will. Then I called my agent to tell him to book me on anything he could, because I was going to need to make a lot of money as fast as I could. I told Greenie that I "had an emergency," but I didn't tell him what it was. I explained, "I need to work, and I don't care where it is."

Greenie answered, "You want to go to Taipei? I have an offer from there on my desk right now." So, I flew to Taipei to make "Mob Busters" with Richard Keil.

After a few weeks overseas, I returned home to a surprising phone call. It was someone from my pathology lab who said, "Misty, I don't know how to tell you this, but we have made a mistake. You are not terminal. You are not at stage 4. You are only at stage 2, and we can treat this thing!"

My doctor told me all the options again and we decided that I would still go ahead and have surgery to remove my thyroid. A short time before surgery, my phone rang, and it was Hugh Hefner's secretary Mary, saying, "Misty, Hef heard you were going to have surgery." I hadn't seen Hef in quite a while, and I was quite surprised he had found out about my operation, especially when I had been keeping it very quiet.

Mary continued, "Hef thinks you should use the Playboy plastic surgeon to do the open and close for your operation." So, I arranged for Dr. Steve Hoefflin to assist with my surgery. Afterward, he touched me up and no one would know I had ever had my throat cut open.

My operation was at Cedar Sinai hospital and since my surgery was very early in the morning, they asked me to check in to the hospital just before midnight.

But since I had been trying to make all the money I could, I had booked myself to judge a Mr. America contest that night. Of course, I wore my favorite red sequined dress. My friend Michael Hewitson drove me to the event. (Can you imagine me driving my own car as I try to step on the gas and brake, while I'm in my skin-tight evening gown?)

But the contest ran long. I kept asking what time it was. I knew I needed to be at the hospital by midnight. When it finally ended, we had to drive straight to the hospital, and I walked into the lobby at midnight, still wearing my sparkly, red dress. I told the nurse at the desk, "I'm here." She smiled and replied, "You sure are."

Before they put me to sleep, I had to sign papers stating that if needed, they could clip my vocal nerve. If something went wrong, I might never talk again, so it was very scary.

My surgery was supposed to take two hours. It took nine. When I woke up, I saw my parents standing over my bed. I couldn't talk, but when the surgeon came in, he informed us that mine was the largest thyroid he'd ever taken out of a woman. It was the size of a small papaya, and it was strangling me.

The surgery was a complete success, but a few days after I was home, a new problem arose. My hair started to fall out. I had a huge bald spot on the rear top part of my head. In a panic, I called my doctor. He assured me it was nothing serious. It turned out to be caused by the combination of all the stress I had been under, and the nine hours they had pushed the back of my head down on the table when they were operating on me.

I still had the big bald spot when I went for my follow-up procedure with Dr. Hoefflin. As I laid down on his operating table, he could tell that I was scared. Dr. Hoefflin said, "Misty, I have a surprise for you. Close your eyes."

The door opened and I heard someone walk in. Dr. Hoefflin said, "Misty, this is Michael. He's going to sing you to sleep." I opened my eyes and was staring straight up into the beautiful eyes of Michael Jackson! Dr. Hoefflin later explained that he had been Michael's plastic surgeon.

The doctor started the IV drop into my arm and Michael asked, "What would you like me to sing to you?" I was instantly woozy, and I could only come up with, "Do you know anything by Kenny Rogers?" Michael giggled and said, "How about 'We Are the World?' I sang that one with Kenny." Before he got through the first line, I was out.

When I came to, Michael was gone, and so was my thyroid operation scar.

FAIRYTALE WEDDING…
NIGHTMARE DIVORCE

On a summer day of 1985, I was running late for my acting class at Stella Adler's. If I had been on time, my life would have taken a completely different direction.

I walked into class, 5 minutes late, and saw all the seats were taken. One young man quickly stood up and offered me his chair. Nine months later, I married that man. His name was James DePaiva. Later, when I told him I thought he had been such a gentleman to offer me his chair that day, Jim admitted, "I was there on scholarship and we had been instructed that when a paying student came in, we had to give them our seat."

Like me, when he started at Stella's, Jim had very little money. But when he shared his dream of being an actor with Stella, she allowed him to attend on a scholarship, as long as he ran the sound and lights for her.

When he wasn't in acting class, Jim was waiting tables. I could tell he was broke just by looking at him. His shoes had big holes in them. I learned later that he lived in a government subsidized building and slept on a futon.

Jim was very shy when we first met. But once we got to know each other in class, he asked me out. Since he had no money, we went bicycle riding on the beach. On his birthday, when I gave him a wrapped present, he said, "It looks like a shoebox." When he opened it, he found a new pair of Nikes. He cuddled them like a baby and said, "These are the nicest shoes I've ever had. They are almost too nice to wear." I said, "You are wearing them! Throw away those that have the holes in them."

Jim and I started going together, and one day in acting class, we shared a memorable scene. It was from "Cat on a Hot Tin Roof." James was on a bed and I was supposed to seduce him. I was wearing just a slip as I walked over to him. But a few lines into it, Stella stopped me and yelled, "Misty, you are too sweet! No man will ever marry you if you act that sweet. You need to take control. This woman wants a baby with this man. You make that man do what you want him to do."

I started again, doing as Stella had instructed. The sweet Misty was gone, replaced by a much more powerful and sexy woman. Jim apparently liked what he saw in that scene, because a short time later, in real life, he asked me to marry him! I told him "No." My turning him down had nothing to do with him being a waiter who made next to nothing. I just wanted to make sure that we were both truly in love. But for the next month, Jim asked me to marry him, at least ten times a day! I finally gave in and said "Yes."

When I announced our engagement to my Hee Haw family, Lulu Roman gave me a wedding shower in the Kornfield. All my Hee Haw family did everything they could to give me the wedding I had always dreamed of. Marianne and Kenny Rogers arranged for us to get married at their church in Westwood. Kenny also gave me a priceless wedding gift. He took my official wedding portrait. You can see it in the photo section of this book.

Marianne and Kenny had me stay overnight at their home the night before the wedding. Before I went to bed, Marianne said, "Misty, you know you need to wear something borrowed and something blue tomorrow." Then she put around my neck, the most magnificent necklace I had ever seen. It had diamonds and pearls and a huge sapphire in the middle. After we took our wedding photos, Jim made me give the necklace back to Marianne before we left for our honeymoon. I told her, "Jim said he would be up all night making sure no one broke in and stole that."

Marianne was my matron of honor, Barbie Benton was my bridesmaid, and Mary Jo, my best friend from high school was my maid of honor. Our wedding was the second of the day at the Methodist church. When they found out we would have no flowers at the altar, because we had very little money, a church official asked the first wedding party if they would leave their flowers up for our wedding!

Jim and I were married on April 6, 1986. As my daddy prepared to walk me down the aisle, Marianne Rogers went before us. Christopher, Marianne and Kenny's little boy, started screaming for her as she walked by him. When she got to the altar, Marianne turned around and told him to be quiet. Today, Marianne jokes that Christopher was trying to warn me that I was making a big mistake!

Sam Lovullo let us hold our wedding reception in his new, $5,000,000 home, and his wife Grace decorated her whole house and furnished our cake. Our wedding really was perfect, even on our limited budget. Our honeymoon was also low-cost. We spent just one night at the Bel Air Hotel in Beverly Hills, and that was thanks to a fan of Hee Haw. Don Wilkins was very well-to-do, and he loved Hee Haw. He came to all the tapings and when he found out I was going to get married, he said he wanted to give us the night at the Bel Air as his gift.

To say that our marriage was quite an adventure would be an understatement. When we got married, I was the "breadwinner" and "star" of the family. I was enjoying my highest popularity on Hee Haw, and was also making appearances on other TV shows and movies. Jim continued to wait tables, as he went on auditions, hoping to get his own break into show business.

That break came just one year into our marriage. Jim managed to get a major audition, even though he didn't have a demo reel or anything on tape that he could show them.

Jim found a play script that I had written called "Just Another Blonde." He thought it was really good, and he asked to use a scene from it for his audition.

The casting director for ABC said, "You are fantastic Jim. We would like to fly you to New York for a screen test for "One Life to Live."

My friend, Faye Sloan, was working as a wardrobe designer for Universal Studios at the time. When I told her about Jim's upcoming screen test, she said, "We need to bulk him up and turn him into a hunk." Since he wasn't that big and muscular, Faye gave him an undershirt, with a plaid shirt and then a vest on top of that.

As James made the long flight from Los Angeles to New York City, I prayed that he would do well. And he did. Ten other men had screen-tested for the same role, but James is the one who got it. He was hired to play the part of Max Holden on 'One Life to Live," and it would change our lives forever…for better and for worse.

People throw around the phrase "overnight success." But my husband truly was one. He went from waiting tables in California one day to being a television soap opera star in New York City the very next day. Jim became the new "soap hunk." He became famous almost instantly. Of course, I wanted to be near my husband, so I leased out the Hollywood Hills home I had lived in for the past decade, and Jim and I got a condo in New York.

For the next 16 years, Jim was on all the covers of the soap opera magazines, posing with his latest leading lady. When he showed me his first paycheck, I was overjoyed that I was no longer the "bread winner." Jim could have bought his own bread bakery! The money he was pulling in from that TV show was incredible. While Jim worked on his show, I continued working on mine. I didn't mind at all, that Jim's weekly salary was more than I was making all year on Hee Haw.

But I did get a major bonus when Robin Leach made a guest appearance on Hee Haw. Robin was known for his show "Lifestyles of the Rich and Famous," but we had met when I was promoting "Goodbye Norma Jean" at the Cannes Film Festival. After his Hee Haw taping, Robin surprised me when he said, "Misty, I'm going to send you and your husband on a trip. I'd like you to be on my show "Runaway with the Rich and Famous."

It was probably the greatest vacation of my life. We went to Quebec, where they had the Royal Guard come out to march for us. We stayed in a castle for four days and had our own butler who served us 10 different kinds of tea. When we went out to dinner, we went in a Rolls Royce, and I drove a yacht down the St. Lawrence River. As they instructed me how to steer the yacht, I joked, "This is just like the truck pulls!"

We sailed over to a little island to have lunch at a beautiful waterfall. When the TV show aired, viewers thought that was how we spent all our vacations! It was all very elegant and romantic. So romantic, that when I came back home, I was pregnant. I was so excited as I prepared to have a baby. I had no second thoughts about putting my career as a "sex symbol" on hold.

I was 5 ½ months along when I went to the doctor for an ultrasound. James went with me. He said he would read his next day's script while he waited in the room with me. Halfway through the procedure, the sonographer paused and said, "I will be right back." As I lay there, I began to worry that something might be wrong, but I didn't say anything to Jim, as he continued to silently read his script.

When a doctor walked in and started looking at the monitor, my nervousness increased. My worst fears were confirmed when the doctor said, "Your baby is swollen. There is water around the baby's heart, and I don't think the baby is going to make it."

Jim suddenly dropped his script as he looked at the face of his terrified wife. They did more tests and then decided that they should abort the baby. I told them I could not do that. The doctor explained, "It would be best if we took it out." I said, "It's little heart is still beating, and I will carry it as long as God wants me to."

I went home and kept my word. I had that baby's body inside me until one night I woke up and I was just shaking. I screamed to Jim and said, "My Grandma Sophie was here, and she took the baby!" Jim said, "What are you talking about. Your grandma died when you were 13." I said, "I felt my grandma in the room, and she took the baby."

I went to the doctor the next day and the baby had no heartbeat. I had to go to the hospital, but "One Life to Live" told Jim that he could only have two hours off to take me. Our life quickly turned into a soap opera as I had complications and almost bled to death during the procedure to take the baby out. Once I survived that, I became very sick. The doctor explained that the toxins from the deceased baby I had kept inside me had poisoned me. My skin broke out in hives, 200 to 300 at first, and then over 1, 000.

I was put on prednisone and that made me swell up like a balloon. I was quite a sight. I lost the baby in February, and I went into a deep depression. I had lost my looks, my health and most of all, my baby.

I didn't think it was right for a baby to pass from this world and not have a name, so I named our baby "Paul." A few months after the death of my child, as the June Hee Haw taping approached, I tried to pull myself together. I was feeling better physically, but emotionally and mentally, I was still struggling.

Before our first shoot, I was sitting quietly in the dressing room, when Minnie Pearl walked in. She hugged me tightly and said, "I heard you lost your baby. But you are young, and I want you to try again." Then Minnie poured out her heart, "You know, Henry and I always wanted children. But the Lord didn't have that in our plan. I remember seeing someone with a baby carriage and I would run home and cry and cry. But I always dried my tears before Henry came home, because I didn't want him to see me crying." Then Minnie pulled me close and whispered, "I am going to pray that you can have a baby." I never forgot Minnie's kind words.

In his own effort to lift my spirits, Hee Haw's producer Sam Lovullo planned a very special surprise for me.

Sam got together with The Nashville Network's Charlie Chase, who was filming a "Candid Camera" type show called "Funny Business." During the show, Charlie played practical jokes on different country music celebrities. Sam and Charlie came up with a plan to prank me.

We were filming our "All Jug Band" skit on Hee Haw and the script called for "Hee Haw Hunk" Jeff Smith to be in a gorilla suit as he flirted with me. But in the middle of the skit, they secretly switched Jeff with my husband, whom they had flown into Nashville from California.

The entire time we filmed the skit, I thought Jeff was in the gorilla outfit, but it was really my husband. As the cameras rolled, I noticed the gorilla getting a little bit "too handsy." I couldn't imagine Jeff was feeling me up in front of everyone. As he got more and more aggressive, I finally slapped him and then I ripped his gorilla head right off...only to look right into the face of my own husband!

Sam was right, it did lift my spirits. It had been a very long time since I had laughed as hard as I did that day.

I also got a little bit of payback when Jim appeared in the Gossipy Girls skit. As he was singing the last note of the song with the other girls, I got a cream-filled pie and hit him right in the face. As the crew howled with laughter, Jim grabbed me and gave me a big kiss to make sure we were both covered with whipped cream.

In 1990, Jim was one of the most popular actors on daytime TV. After three years on the soap opera, he wanted to see if he could become an even bigger star in Hollywood. James left "One Life to Live," and the show hired another actor to take his place. To explain the change, the writers came up with a story about Max Holden needing plastic surgery. James and I moved back to my home in Hollywood. We also bought a little cabin at Lake Arrowhead.

But we quickly learned that Jim's soap opera popularity could also be a drawback. When he tried to get other roles, he found that he had been typecast as his Max Holden character. No one would hire him, and in one year, he went from making $850, 000 to less than $1, 000.

I decided to sell my Hollywood Hills home and we bought one in Topanga Canyon. But after a year, the producer of "One Life to Live" asked Jim to come back to the show. When he returned, there was no mention of why or how the two Max Holdens had suddenly swapped places again. Only in the soap operas!

The celebrity tabloids and soap opera magazines love "celebrity couples," so they ran articles and photos of us almost every week. When we first got married, James got a lot of publicity because I was a "star." Now that he was the ABC network's number one daytime hunk, I received a lot of publicity because of him. We said yes to every interview and photo shoot request we got. We both enjoyed all the attention, and boy, were we about to get some attention!

A few years after losing my first child, I found myself pregnant again. My due date was a month after my 42nd birthday.

I spent most of my pregnancy at our home in Los Angeles, while Jim stayed at our old condo across the country in New York, while he worked on "One Life to Live." The one disadvantage to being on a soap opera, is that you get almost no time off. They work five days a week, 50 weeks a year. But he was able to arrange a two-week vacation once our baby was born.

Los Angeles in the summer of 1992 was a scary place for a mother-to-be. The L.A. riots were raging after the Rodney King-police beating verdict. Ironically, as I am writing this, similar riots are taking place in Los Angeles and across the entire country. Sadly, it seems that some things never change.

Since I was now three years older than I was when I lost my first child, this was considered a high-risk pregnancy, and the doctors kept a very-close watch on me throughout the nine months. But my main obstetrician put me at ease during the week I turned 42, when he walked into the examining room and smiled, "How is the most beautiful pregnant woman in the universe?"

Leading up to the due date, we had planned that Jim would fly in to be my coach during the birth. Mary Jo, my best friend from high school would also be there to videotape it all. (Hey, we were a TV family! My daughter might as well start early!)

But all those plans changed when I went into labor on July 2nd. I called a friend, Joe Morales and asked him to drive me to the hospital, which was usually a 45-minute drive from my home…except today. Because of all of the street closings and detours because of the riots, it seemed that every road Joe took ended up being closed. As my contractions grew closer, Joe made me laugh as he yelled, "Not in my car!" and "I'm a banker. I don't know nothing about birthin' no babies!"

When we finally arrived at Cedars-Sinai, Mary Jo told me that Jim was still on the plane, flying from New York City. I told my doctor, "I don't want the baby to come out until Jim is here." Dr. Rice said, "That baby is coming now. It's not important that the father be here at the birth. It's important that he be here for your child's next 18 years."

With Jim still up in the air, Mary Jo said she would be my coach. But now we needed someone to videotape everything. Mary called my friend Steven Rubin, whom we had already named to be our child's Godfather. Steven was also a rabbi. When she told him our request that he film the birth, he gave a flat, "No way. That is too much for me." Steven's wife Didi cried, "You big wimp!", as she headed out the door to become our videographer. But my doctor had one last instruction before I began my most important production.

"I have found that the baby bonds so much better with the mother, if you do this," Dr. Rice explained. "When the baby's shoulder comes out and I get the head, I like the mother to reach down and pull the baby out."

I was horrified! I screamed, "Oh no! I can't do that." But he insisted, "When the time comes, you try this, because you will have such power in that child's life. If you can pull your own baby out, you can do anything."

Guess what. I did it! I named that baby Dreama. Dreama means "Hope." After all the riots, it was my hope that there would be a better world, and I had brought this child into it, hoping that she would brighten the world. She had already brightened mine.

Broadway star Joy Franz, a friend of mine, came to the hospital and sang to Dreama. And Dreama's biggest fan also walked in. Jim finally arrived from New York, and he couldn't wait to hold his baby girl. It was the happiest day of our lives.

Leading up to Dreama's birth, I had already decided that I was going to put my TV and movie career on hold (maybe forever), so I could stay home and be a full-time mother. My last TV role was in an episode of the CBS series "MacGyver." I had an extremely dramatic part in the show. I thought it was a good role to end on.

For the majority of our marriage, Jim and I lived 3, 000 miles apart. I missed being with my husband in person, but I could see him each day on TV. As I watched him do his (very frequent) love scenes with his lucky co-stars, I always looked forward to the next weekend when we could be together.

Once Dreama was born, I began making plans to move to New York, so we could be together like a normal family. As I put my California home on the market, I thought back to how hard I had worked to get the money for that home. As soon as the sale was final, I packed up my baby and we headed east to our new life in the Big Apple.

Our condo in New York was close to Jim's job, but it was pretty small for our growing family. In addition to our new baby, we also had two dogs and a cockatoo. Jim wanted us to buy another home, and he had always dreamed of owning a huge stone home.

We found the home of Jim's dreams in Ridgefield, Connecticut. It was so huge, it was almost ridiculous. It was a 13, 000 square feet,

14 room house that had 9 fireplaces and 92 windows! It also had two apartments for staff. The asking price was $1,650,000. We offered a million dollars, and it was turned down. Then, I called my psychic friend Karen Prisant, and asked her how high we should go. She said, "Offer them $1,048,000 and 12 cents." I asked, "Why the 12 cents?" Karen laughed, "They will also ask you why the 12 cents, and you will be able to say, 'Because that is every penny we have. We can't go one cent higher.'"

And that's exactly what happened. They accepted our second offer, including our last 12 cents. While the mansion was my husband's idea, I was the one who provided the $400,000 down payment. It was all my life savings and all the money I had made from the sale of my California home. But I looked at it as an investment in my family. Unfortunately, it was an investment that wouldn't pay off.

Almost as soon as we moved into his dream home, Jim began to change. He would get moody and he started to spend more and more time at his condo in New York. He got to where he would spend at least three nights a week there, while I was in our 13,000 square foot home with a one-year old baby. What I thought was going to be our dream home, had quickly turned into one lonely mansion.

One day, my sister-in-law Wanda had dropped in and she turned on "One Life to Live", joking, "Let's see what Jim is up to today."

At the exact moment we tuned in, Jim was starting a love scene with a new girl who had joined the show. We both sat, almost stunned as the scene played out. I had done lots of similar scenes in movies, but there was something different about this. Wanda looked at me and said, "That is not acting. Something is going on there."

As Jim's trips home became less frequent, when he did show up, he was usually in a foul mood. I naively thought his hostility was due to being overworked. He was always having to be on the set early or having to shoot late at night. At least that's the excuse he gave for not wanting to come home overnight.

One evening, when he did come home, Jim announced, "I got into therapy. I was becoming a mean man, and I didn't like who I was becoming. I think you should also go to a therapist." I wanted to go to marriage counseling together, but Jim declined. So, I said I would be glad to see a therapist by myself. I was willing to do anything to get us back to being our happy, loving family again. But to be honest, I don't think Jim's was getting his money's worth from his therapist, because every time he came home, his mood was darker than ever before.

Our life had seemed like a dream. We had everything. Fame and fortune, a beautiful baby, and an unbelievable home. Then our life fell apart, and my life was going to go lower than it had ever been.

I met Jim for lunch at Jack Sprat's restaurant in New York. Our baby girl was sitting at the table with us when…out of the blue…Jim coldly stated, "I'm divorcing you, and you should get a lawyer." Then he took another bite of linguine. Of course, my response was the classic, "Is there someone else?" He quickly answered, "No. I just want to live by myself and play my guitar. The house and the baby and everything are too much."

As soon as he left, I went to the phone and called my psychic friend Karen. Karen was not a party psychic. She was a professional. She worked for the FBI, and she had found kidnapped children and helped locate bodies of murder victims. She was very powerful. As soon as I asked her why my husband was leaving me, she advised me to contact the husband of my husband's new-favorite co-star Kassie Wesley.

After a little searching, I found Richard's number and when he answered, I introduced myself, "My name is Misty Rowe, and I think my husband is dating your wife." Richard replied, "Well, now it all makes sense."

Richard told me his wife had asked for a divorce a couple months earlier, the day before their 6th wedding anniversary. Richard was now living in their home in California, while he worked on "NYPD Blue." Of course, like me, he was now going through the lowest point in his life. But after the initial shock from my call wore off, Richard asked if I wanted to work together with him to see what we could find out about our cheating spouses.

The first thing we checked was our phone bills. Richard said, "Here's a number that my wife has called a hundred times." I said, "Yep, that is my husband's. We continued our investigation and began putting all the pieces of our very sad puzzle together.

About that time, Marianne Rogers called and when I answered, she happily asked, "How is that big beautiful house and that gorgeous baby and your handsome husband?" I tearfully answered, "Well, the big, beautiful house is for sale, the baby is with me and the husband has run off." Marianne was stunned. But after a few moments, she advised me to get the best lawyer I could afford.

About this time, I had a conversation with my Hee Haw pal Roni Stoneman. Roni was the stick-thin, gap toothed, banjo-playing ball of fire, who played the unhappily married Ida Lee Nagger on the show. When Roni heard about my marriage troubles, she said, "Let me tell you what I did Misty."

Oh, and I forgot to tell you that you should never mess with Roni in any way. "My husband wanted a divorce and the judge said he could get 50% of everything we had," Roni said, as she grew more and more animated. "He came to get his half, and I met him at the front door with a chainsaw. As he stepped in, I took that chainsaw to our coffee table. I yelled over the roar of the motor, "There's your 50%! What else do you want?"

Roni was prepared to saw every piece of their furniture in half. I told her I didn't think I was quite as proficient with a chainsaw, but I was hopeful that James and I could work everything out in a civil, fair and friendly manner. For some reason, Roni slapped her knee, as she doubled over with laughter.

After hiring a good lawyer, I put our huge mansion up for sale. Of course, just like Roni Stoneman had warned me, Jim wanted his half of the money from the sale, even though most of the over $400,000 we had put into it, was from my own money I had made before we were married.

When we started our divorce proceedings, the first question I was asked was, "Why do you deserve any kind of alimony?" I told the judge, "Look at all the zeros on my husband's paycheck. I gave up my career to raise our child. My family and career are in California and Nashville, and to be there for my husband, I now live in a part of the country where I know no one."

My brother Ed was so mad. He told me, "When you met Jim, he had nothing. He had nothing, but now he has everything, and he's going to leave you with nothing because you paid for that huge mansion with your money, but you let him put his name on it."

Dividing up our money was less emotional than dividing up the time we would spend with our daughter. When the judge ruled that Jim could be with Dreama every other weekend, I spoke up and said, "He can see his daughter anytime he wants to. I would like an open-door policy. If he wants to come be with his child on Christmas, I'm totally OK with him being there." My lawyer grabbed my arm and tried to stop me, but I continued, "He is welcome anytime. I don't want my daughter growing up without a father."

About that time, Jim moved his direct deposit to a different bank. With me without a job, it didn't take long for my bank account to dwindle down to nothing, while the monthly bills quickly piled up.

While we waited for an offer on the house, my mother moved in with me. She was a big help in caring for my two-year-old, but she was also helping take care of me. I had stopped eating, and I lost 12 pounds in one month. I went to put on a pair of jeans and they just fell off, and the stress of an upcoming court deposition had destroyed any appetite I had.

It was stressful enough when I had to answer lots of prying questions. But I had no idea what was coming when my husband started answering his questions. I was about to get to know Jim in a way I never had before.

My lawyer asked, "While married, have you had sexual intercourse with anyone other than Misty?" Jim answered, "Yes," and my lawyer asked for their names. I sat, totally speechless, as he listed seven names. One was his co-star, whom he left me for. I knew six of the women and had even made dinner for one in our home. The one I had never heard of was a woman he had a fling with, in the back of a limo.

And the hits kept on coming when my lawyer asked Jim, "During those encounters, did you use protection?" His lawyer objected, saying, "James has a right to privacy, and you are not entitled to that answer."

I was in such a state of shock. I had never been so hurt. My heartache grew when I remembered the date. It was our nine-year anniversary. When I left the court that day, I went out and got my own anniversary present…an AIDS test.

By the time, I got to the parking lot, my hurt was now being overtaken by anger. I was in such a fury, and I was about to make a move that would make Roni Stoneman proud.

I called Richard, the man whose wife was cheating on him with my husband. I said, "Richard, I think our spouses deserve each other. But I think before we tell them goodbye, we should have a little fun."

The court ruled that Jim could come visit with Dreama every other weekend. But he wanted it to be at our big house, so while he stayed there for two days, I went to our old condo, the one he was still living at. (Here's a tip for all stupid men. Never let your soon-to-be ex-wife stay at your condo while you aren't there.)

One weekend, I walked into his bedroom and there was a tube of K-Y jelly next to the bed. I took the jelly to the medicine cabinet, where I found a tube of Ben-Gay. I sat on the couch and called Richard, saying, "Richard, you won't believe what I'm doing right now…"

I squeezed out all the jelly, then I got a chopstick and dipped it into the Ben-Gay. Using that chopstick, I was able to fill up that old tube of jelly with the Ben-Gay. I cleaned it all off and put it right back by the bed. For the very first time, I was now looking forward to the next romantic night for my husband and his lover! I bet it turned into a real hot time!

Can you believe that the next time I had to appear in court, Jim's lawyer accused me of "bodily harm'? When I admitted to exchanging the K-Y for the Ben-Gay, I said, "It was a joke…and I guess he got it." The judge had to turn completely around in his big chair, so we wouldn't see him laughing. The bailiff was visibly biting his tongue, and then the stenographer who was typing all the notes on the case, looked up and asked, "How do you spell K-Y?" My husband's lawyer knew he wasn't going to get his "bodily harm".

I called Richard and it made his day when I told him how my prank turned out. He said, "I have an idea that might be just as good, but we will need to meet in person."

Through all our ordeal, Richard and I had only spoken by phone. But we made plans to meet for dinner the next time I made it out to California. A short time later, I was appearing in the musical "Always...Patsy Cline" in La Mirada, and he came to see the show. Afterward, we went out to dinner and he ordered a bottle of very-expensive champagne. I told him, "That costs too much," but he replied, "Misty, after all the dinners your husband has taken my wife to, I can buy us a bottle of champagne."

At the end of the night, we took a photo of the two of us, both with huge smiles and waving at the camera. I was going to get on with my life and he was too. But first, he had one last trick up his sleeve.

Richard was going to have to leave his country home, and his ex-wife was going to take it over. I wondered why he told me that he couldn't wait for my ex and his ex to spend their first night in his former bedroom. I had no idea what he was up to, but I knew it would be good!

Richard got 50 copies of the photo we had taken together. Then he stapled all those pictures to the bedroom ceiling. He said, "When they lay in bed and look up, they are going to see our big smiles as we look down at them.

Later, Richard took that same photo and turned it into a fancy wine label. He put it on a bottle of my ex-husband's favorite wine and sent it to me for my 50th birthday.

Remember all the attention and publicity Jim and I had received throughout our marriage? We enjoyed every magazine and tabloid story and photo. But I learned the hard way, that once your perfect, happy marriage implodes, those magazines turn into a totally different beast.

Once word of our marriage troubles got out, the press had a field day. I was at the grocery store, standing in line to buy baby food for my two-year-old, when I saw a photo of my husband on a magazine cover, with a headline talking about his "new love."

The National Enquirer repeatedly called my home phone, and when I answered, a reporter asked, "What do you think about your husband dating Kassie?" Imagine that. What would be your answer? What would you think about your husband or wife dating someone else? We weren't even divorced yet. Did the reporter think I would be thrilled for them? The only response I could think of, was Cathy Baker's famous Hee Haw sign-off of "That's all," as I slammed down the phone. Then I sat at my kitchen table and cried for the next half hour.

Neither James nor I had any privacy at all, as the sordid details of our divorce were dragged through the press. I joked with Marianne Rogers that the only difference in our divorces, was that hers made the cover of The Star tabloid and mine only made the fourth page. In another issue of The Star, Marianne and I both made the cut for "Hollywood's 100 Dirtiest Divorces."

Going through a divorce is one of the most painful things you can do. When you have to go through it in front of the public, that pain only increases. Another Hee Haw Honey also dealt with that same public humiliation. My friend Kathie Lee Gifford endured a year of tabloid headlines about her husband Frank cheating on her. But thanks to her strong faith, she was able to survive all the negative publicity and late-night comedian jokes, and her marriage survived as well. Kathie Lee and Frank were still married when he passed away in 2015.

After the dust had settled, I had managed to get back my money from the down payment on our home. Jim also paid seven years of alimony and child support.

When marriages end, some people have nice divorces, and some have nasty ones. Mine was a bad one. But my relationship with Jim has improved since our marriage ended in 1996. Even after 25 years, we are still not friends, but we have a truce. I'm so glad we are no longer bitter towards each other, and we never fight.

Four months after our divorce, Jim ended up marrying his co-star, and they have one son, James Quentin. He's Dreama's half-brother, and she loves him very much.

Marianne Rogers once told me, "Who you marry is not as important as who you have a child with. Because once you have a child with someone, you are tied to that person for all of that child's life." She was right.

KICKED OUT OF THE KORNFIELD

In May of 1990, I celebrated my milestone 40th birthday. I was also close to celebrating two decades on Hee Haw. But for some reason, I hadn't received the usual phone call informing me of when I should be in Nashville for our June tapings.

When the phone finally rang, I was relieved to hear Sam Lovullo's voice…until I heard what he had to say.

"Misty, they are scaling down the show, and I'm the one who has to make the calls to let a lot of people go." I could tell that he was broken hearted…almost as much I was. I tried to smile through my tears as I said, "Well, thanks for the memories Sam. It's been a great run."

A week later, I was standing in line in the grocery star, when I looked over at the National Enquirer that had the headline, "Cornfield Massacre." It included a photo of me standing on top of a hay wagon. That tabloid story detailed how I was one of a number of 40-plus year old women fired from the show. Cathy Baker,

Gunilla Hutton, Ronnie Stoneman and my best friend Marianne Rogers were also let go. To take our place, the show hired fresher faced, perkier breasted 25-year-old girls that no one had ever heard of. Cathy Baker immediately said, "We should sue them."

Cathy and none of the other girls followed through with a lawsuit, but I was convinced that this was totally wrong, and probably illegal. My husband told me, "It will probably cost a lot to fight them. But if you feel you have been discriminated against for any reason, you have every right to use the money from this marriage to get justice."

I went to a law firm and met with a big group of lawyers to see if they'd take my case. After looking over all my financial papers and contracts, they said, "You have a merchandising contract with the show. Did you get anything from the sales of T-shirts, calendars or lunch boxes?" I answered, "Not one dollar. I even modeled the Hee Haw jackets in their magazine ads, but I never got a cent."

The lawyers told me I should actually be suing for that money first. But I would have had to pay for a complete audit of the show, and that would have cost me $35, 000 that I didn't have. I ended up dropping that case, but my legal team was confident that my age discrimination suit was a stronger case.

But there was one big problem. In addition to suing the Gaylord Corporation, I would also have to sue Sam Lovullo. Papa Sam. The man who had been like an uncle or second father to me. I told my lawyers I couldn't sue Sam. But they insisted, explaining, "Unless you file suit against Sam, you will never get to Gaylord. He's the one who hired you and he's the one who signed all your contracts."

I was sick, and heartbroken. I'm sure Sam was as well. When I signed the lawsuit papers, I cried. People said, "Oh, my God, I can't believe you sued Sam." Joan Kovats, my equity agent, warned me, "If you sue them, you will never work in this town again." I answered, "This will continue until someone has the guts to take a stand."

When I told my older brother that I was going to sue the Gaylord company, Eddie laughed at me. He asked, "Who do you think you are? You're a little girl who's going to stand up to one of the largest corporations in America." He continued, "Women get old and they get fired. Deal with it." I answered, "This is something I have to do. I just had a baby girl, and if her mother is afraid to stand up now, she will grow up and have to deal with the same crap."

My brother was right about one thing. I didn't have any power. But I did have a brilliant lawyer who advised me to go to the Equal Employment Opportunity Center. I had just had my baby who was now two weeks old. I stood in line at the EEOC in the courtroom in downtown Los Angeles and as I waited, I was surrounded by people who had been discriminated against for age, sex, or race.

After giving them all my paperwork, they transferred my case to their Nashville office, where a nice man named Clarence prepared to pay a visit to the management at the Gaylord company.

Clarence walked into the Gaylord office and said to the bosses, "I have an age discrimination complaint from Misty Rowe, and my advice to you is to give Misty Rowe what she wants." The Gaylord brass all laughed. Clarence continued, "After being on the show 19 years, you fired her, along with some other women who were all in their 40s, and I have the names of all the new girls you hired to replace them." The Gaylord bosses laughter stopped when Clarence explained, "If those new women are in their 20s, you're a$$ is grass, and you're not going to like what happens next, because age discrimination is no longer legal."

Clarence drove back to his office, but before he got there, the Gaylord higher ups had faxed a settlement offer to my lawyer. Clarence was disappointed that I took the settlement. He was convinced I could have gotten much more. He also said if all the girls had banded together, he would have taken the case to Federal Court and the payoff would have been much, much higher. I could have fought for more, but I ended up buying a real big house with that settlement money.

I had stood up for myself, and I had won. But I also paid a very high price. To say the least, it did not make me popular. Of course, I became a pariah to the Gaylord Corporation, and no one from Hee Haw would talk to me. No one. I talked to those who had been let go, but the ones still left had nothing to do with me.

But eventually, as time went on, people began to heal. As new people replaced the old ones at Gaylord, people seemed to forgive and forget. I don't think the people I dealt with are there anymore. But it would still be many years before Sam Lovullo spoke to me again. Five years, to be exact.

By then, I was divorced, living in a small home in Greenwich, Connecticut. For some reason, I picked up the phone and dialed Sam's number. When he picked up, I quietly said, "Hi Sam, it's Misty."

After a long pause, he gruffly asked, "What do you want?" I answered, "Sam, I don't want anything. I just wanted to say hello and see how you were doing." When he realized I truly didn't want anything except to reconnect with him, he slowly warmed up to me. At the end of our conversation, he said we would talk again sometime soon.

That "sometime soon" turned out to be ten years later.

DREAMA AND ROSIE

I have written a lot about all the TV shows and movies I've been in. But there is one special film that you probably haven't seen. I kind of hope you haven't, but if you have, I hope it was a blessing to you.

My friends Steven and Didi Reuben had been working with a foundation called griefHaven. It was founded by Susan Whitmore for parents who had lost a child. The child may have been murdered, died in an accident, had cancer, or something else. It didn't matter how the child died, the pain for the parents was the same. The foundation was making a film in which parents shared their stories and their grief.

They asked to interview me for the project, but I said, "My child was never born, so some people wouldn't see it as a child. They just think of it as a lost pregnancy." But Susan assured me, "When a woman loses a baby, she can have grief for a very long time, with a lot of that grief hidden deep inside her.

Naomi Watts narrated the documentary film called "Portraits of Hope: The Parent's Journey." Hopefully, you have never seen it and never will, because the only people allowed to see it are parents who have lost a child. Today, more than one million people a year visit the griefHaven.org website.

I agreed to do their documentary so that I could give some hope to other parents. Because after my first child died, my second one lived. After all my grief, I found joy like I had never known before.

I was completely devastated when my marriage ended. But I knew that one amazing thing came out of that marriage…my daughter.

Dreama was my dream come true. Dreama is the one who really pushed me to write this book. For a couple years, she kept saying, "Mom you need to tell your story." But when I called and told her, I had started writing it, she changed her tune, saying, "Oh Mom, don't say anything embarrassing!" I laughed, "Well, if I don't say anything embarrassing, it's going to be a short book!" I told her she couldn't have it both ways. So here you go Dreama…your very own chapter. I hope it's not too embarrassing!

My divorce was final, and the challenge of being a single mom was just beginning. After what seemed like an eternity, I was finally able to sell our big mansion, at a loss. Dreama and I moved into a little cottage in Greenwich, Connecticut. Kathie Lee Gifford and Regis Philbin both had big mansions a few miles away, but I liked to say that I was on "the poor side of town."

I guess you could say that we downsized a little, as we went from a 14-room home that had six bedrooms and six baths to our new two bedroom and two-bath cottage. But there was also a little pool house in the backyard, and I would renovate it and add a bathroom and a little kitchenette, so Mama could live there.

On our third night in our new home, Mom was in Dreama's bedroom. They were getting ready for bed and were saying goodnight to the dog I had gotten from Mariska Hargitay. Mariska was the star of "Law & Order SVU," and she's Jayne Mansfield's daughter. When I was Mariska's next-door neighbor, in Hollywood Hills, she gave me her dog. When I moved across the country, I brought the German Shepherd with me.

At 3 a.m., over the barking of our dog, I heard my mom yell for me to call 9-1-1. A man was pounding on the glass of my daughter's room. He was trying to break the glass, when our dog went crazy trying to get at him. My mom was right behind our dog, and between the two of them, they scared the man away.

Our small home had been built in 1930. It had no kitchen cabinets, but it did have one thing that Regis Philbin's mansion didn't have…rats! Since the cottage sat right on the Byram River, the river rats were continually coming into my kitchen. Luckily, I had my mother to help me fight off the rats. I used to joke that I was the perfect date for any man who has had a fantasy about being with two women…since I lived with my mother!

Greenwich was a great place to raise a child, and I quickly found that my all-time favorite role was that of a full-time mom. I fixed breakfast each morning, got Dreama up and ready, and then took her to school. At the end of the day, I'd pick her up, then we'd have a snack and play in our living room. Dreama's friends would often come over for a playdate, and I'd join in as they sang and danced to the latest silly song they had made up. When I was growing up, my mother always had such a great imagination and I tried to entertain my daughter the way my mother had entertained me.

Once Dreama started school, I helped her with her homework. But like many parents, I found that once she got into third grade math, it became too difficult for me, so I hired a tutor to take over. Today, she is very, very smart. Dreama started working with a computer when she was five, and today she is very high tech. Her mom is not. We didn't have laptops in Kornfield Kounty!

I read books to Dreama every night, and I would act out the stories. When she went into kindergarten, I volunteered to read to the children. I read to all the kindergarten classes, and I became a master storyteller. I occasionally dressed up as different characters as I read, and I found that I really enjoyed working with children. I eventually made a TV pilot for a children's show called "Misty's Moo Town," and that led to a TV show called "Misty's Magical Mountain Top."

I created and hosted "Misty's Magical Mountain Top", which some described as a more educational "Pee Wee Herman Show." We built a magic cottage in my front yard, and Noel Blanc, one of the first men I met in Hollywood, was the voice of our magic phone on the show.

We shot most of the shows around the Big Bear Lake area, including at their zoo, library and a Special Olympics event. The show encouraged children to use their imagination and read, and it featured children of all ages and races.

As she was growing up, Dreama was able to experience many things and places that a lot of children don't get to do. She rode in the Disneyland parade with her dad as Disney celebrated soap opera week. She went with me when I performed across the country, from Branson, Missouri to Dallas, Texas. I think all those experiences helped make Dreama the young woman she is today. She loves to travel the world and meet new people.

I wanted to enroll Dreama in dance classes, but I didn't know how we were going to pay for it. But when the woman who owned the dance studio found out I wrote stage productions, she asked me to write a Christmas musical for them. I came up with a wonderful program that featured all the studio dancers and singers, and in return, Dreama was allowed to take dance classes for a year. She took tap and jazz and became a beautiful ballet dancer.

When you become a mom, a lot of your vanity stuff comes to an end. You don't worry so much about your hair, your clothes or what kind of car you drive. I knew my classic '36 Roadster was not good for taking my daughter around town, so I sold it and bought a Jeep. Dreama and I had so many fast food meals in that jeep, that when I went to get it cleaned, the detailer said, "I went to vacuum behind the back seat, and I've never seen so many French fries in my life!"

In late October of 2001, I was hired to direct the production of "Always...Patsy Cline" in Dallas, Texas. Since it was just a month after 9/11, I was scared to fly, so I loaded Dreama and my mom in my Jeep and drove from Greenwich, Connecticut to Dallas.

Dreama was very upset that she wouldn't be home for Halloween. So, the theater manager and the actors in the play that was wrapping its run before we started, all got together and put on their own trick-or-treat just for my daughter. Dreama dressed up in her little witch outfit, and she went up to the snack bar and they loaded her up with all of their candy. Then she went to trick-or-treat the actors in their dressing rooms.

When I did the Groucho Marx Review with Gabe Kaplan at the Sid Ceasar Theater, Dreama dressed up as Groucho, complete with his trademark glasses and cigar. She would also occasionally dress up in the outfit and wig I wore for "Always...Patsy Cline." But my biggest surprise came the day she found the evening gown I wore at the Cannes Film Festival. I was pictured in that gown on so many magazine covers and newspapers, and when she was 8 years old, Dreama got into my closet and put the dress on. She also found my old Marilyn Monroe wig to round out the costume.

Being the child of an actor and actress, you might think that Dreama would want to also go into acting. She does love going to improv classes, but she doesn't aspire to be an actress.

Dreama went to the University of Santa Cruz and graduated on the Dean's list. She has a degree in art and sociology. She is a brilliant artist, and in recent years, she taught English in Japan. She had just returned to the U.S. when the Corona virus broke out. She had gone to visit some friends in Brooklyn when New York went under lockdown. She called her father to come get her, and she spent four months with him at his country home in the Catskills.

Since my daughter is the one who pushed me into writing this book, I thought it was only fair that I pushed her into saying just a few words. I told her she could say absolutely anything about me that she wanted...as long as she began with "I have a really great Mom..."

"I have a really great Mom. She always supported me and let me be who I wanted to be. She has been so resilient throughout her life. She overcame so much to reach the goals she set for herself. When I was little, I didn't understand what a phenomenal career she had.

I loved being with my mother. She was very young at heart, and still is. But there were many times, when she seemed more like a kid than I did. She was always willing to play games and spend time with me. She is really great with any children she encounters.

Mom made my childhood very magical. Her favorite holiday is Christmas, and she always went above and beyond to make Christmas a magical time for me. She would start listening to Christmas music before Halloween, and she covered our house with elaborate decorations. She'd spend over a month decorating, and one Christmas Eve, she asked her boyfriend, Larry DeLuca, to get up on the roof, to make it sound like Santa Claus was at our house.

I definitely had an interesting childhood, thanks to both my mom and dad. I got to experience a lot more than many kids get to. But since both my parents were actors, I think I kind of rebelled against that. When I applied for college, I went as a biology major. That was about as far away from acting as I could get.

I'm so happy Mom has finally written her book. I knew she would. Once she puts her mind to something, she will get it done. I'm thankful I've had a mother who was always proud to be my mom. I am just as proud to be her daughter."

– Dreama DePaiva

At times, when I had to work and couldn't take Dreama with me, my mother was always there to care for her. She also watched her when I would go to the market or run errands.

Dreama, my mother and I lived in our small Greenwich home for seven years. For five of those seven years, I was in therapy, trying to deal with all the anger I felt toward my ex-husband. As I looked at the current state of my life, I could just picture the tabloid magazine headline, "Former Sex Symbol, Now Living a Sad, Lonely Life in Connecticut. "

My therapist told me, "Misty, you have no friends here, you have no career and you're not working. So, I want you to do two things. I want you to take up a hobby, and I want you to work on some kind of project."

For my project, I decided to restore my small cottage, so I could finally have cabinets in the kitchen. I turned it into a wonderful little place, with the help of my contractor Rodger Gibson. As for my hobby, my mother had plans for that. She was very adamant about me starting life over and thought I should get out among adults. But

I didn't know anyone, and after losing my husband and my TV and movie career, I had also lost all of my self-confidence.

My mom had enough confidence for both of us. She had been raised with five brothers during the Great Depression, and she knew no fear. She sternly told me, "You gotta quit being so shy. Next week, you are going line dancing, and I will go with you."

A week later, my sister-in law Wanda watched Dreama as Mom and I went to the Terrace Club. As we watched people line dancing, a woman named Sandi Bria came up and asked, "Aren't you Misty Rowe, Wendy the Car-Hop from Happy Days?"

Sandi and I started visiting, and we became instant friends. She would eventually become Dreama's preschool teacher, and later, she would be my fan club president. But before that, Sandi would tell me that I should give up my show business career.

While I raised my daughter, I continued doing occasional stage plays or musical productions. But those few dates were not enough to pay our bills. I finally had to put our house up for sale. It was then that Sandi very honestly and bluntly announced, "Misty, you have got to get a real job. You've got to take care of your child. You need to give up show business." I whispered, "I don't have any other skills. I didn't go to college, I can't type. I only worked as a waitress on TV."

A few days later, I got a call from a theater in Albany, New York. They were doing a production of "Always...Patsy Cline," and the actress who was playing Louise had to leave because her husband had a heart attack. They asked me to come play the role, so I jumped in my Jeep and took off for New York.

I had done the part of Louise so many times, that I could recite every line in my sleep. It's a good thing, since I was required to walk in and do the musical with no rehearsal at all.

On the second night of the production, my friend Sandi came to see me…just days after she had told me to "get a real job." After the show, while I was out in the lobby, signing autographs, Sandi came running to me. She screamed, "You are a performer, and you are NOT quitting! You were meant to be an entertainer. I see it now. I saw your true talent tonight."

While I wanted to work more, my ex-husband didn't like my daughter missing school to go on the road with me. So, I had to come up with a plan to perform during Dreama's school breaks and vacations. As Dreama did her homework at our kitchen table, I sat down and started to make notes on a couple napkins. That was beginning of my huge "A Misty Christmas" musical production.

If I had to pick the one favorite night of my entire life, I would choose the night that Dreama and my mother Rosie both joined me on stage during my "A Misty Christmas" show in Atlantic City.

I wanted to get the audience involved, so halfway through the show I went out and grabbed a bunch of people and had them take part in a dance contest. Two of the people were my 8-year-old daughter and my 81-year-old mom. I never told the crowd who they were. Mom ended up doing the Michael Jackson moonwalk and the crowd went crazy. I let the crowd choose the dance contest winner and they overwhelmingly chose my mother.

As the crowd applauded, Mom blew kisses to the audience. Later in the show, I did a monologue about how poor we were when I was growing up, but mom always managed to make Christmas so joyful. We had TV cameras filming that entire show, and I am so thankful that we did. I will always treasure the video of that special night, and I'll have more about that video in just a bit.

Mom helped me so much as I was raising my child. When I had to work, Mom was always there to take care of Dreama. When I was doing a play or musical production, whenever possible, I would fly

Dreama and Mom with me. When I wasn't on the road, the three of us would spend our evenings playing games and singing songs.

But when the time came for me to choose between raising my child or going back to a full-time stage, TV and movie career, it really wasn't that hard of a choice to make. When I had to make the same choice, between having my career and taking care of my mother, again, I knew what I needed to do. Today, I do not regret either decision.

My mother was eccentric. She was much more outgoing than I ever was. She was always positive, happy and made friends so easily. But when she was 82 years old, things began to change. Some of her friends started distancing themselves from her, and I didn't know why.

One day, someone knocked on my door and said, "Misty, something's wrong with Rosie. She's acting peculiar." I was with Mom every day, and I hadn't noticed anything. I couldn't see what was happening, but I was about to find out. Mom crashed her car. The accident was so bad that her vehicle ended upside down and the police and fire departments had to use the "jaws of life" to cut her out of the car.

A short time later, I took her to a neurologist for a CAT scan and MRI. Afterward, the doctor called me to sit next to Mom as he asked her a few questions. I was heartbroken when I heard her answers.

"What year is it?" "1942."

"Who is the President?" "Oh, I can't think of his name, but he's on the penny."

My stomach turned inside out. I couldn't believe what I was hearing. She had Alzheimer's Disease. She'd had it for a long time and it was now progressing very quickly. I cared for her as long as I could on my own, but when she walked out of the house at 3 a.m., during a snowstorm, I knew she needed fulltime nursing care.

It is a horrible feeling knowing that the person you love more than anything in the world, the person who gave birth to you, is losing their mind. Mom went with me as I prepared to put her in a nursing facility. She sat beside me as they gave me all the papers to sign. As I read them over, I looked at my mother staring straight ahead. She was smiling, but she didn't know where she was. I started to reconsider and tell them I just couldn't do it. But at that moment, Mom's face changed, and she had a moment of absolute clarity.

She got up and told the woman at the desk, "My daughter doesn't have to sign these admitting papers. I will." She signed her name to each document and checked herself in.

Mom stayed at that location for almost two years, but when I found that they were mistreating her and that she had stopped eating, I decided to move her. My brother Bob is married to a nurse and she worked at a small, skilled nursing facility in California. Lynn put mom on their waiting list, while I sold everything I owned, and prepared to move with Mom to Big Bear Lake. I lived in Big Bear for the decade mom was in that facility. I wanted to be near her, and I also enjoyed being close to my brother again.

My father passed away in 2004, after suffering a couple strokes. Through his life, he never seemed to age. I'm thankful I inherited some of those genes from Dad. I remember him taking me to the county fair and he loved going on all the rides. There was also a booth there with a man who would guess your age. If he missed it by more than 5 years, you won a prize, and they could never come close to my dad's real age. He always looked so much younger than he was.

For ten years, I went to visit my mother at least 3 times a week. The nursing facility allowed me to take her to McDonalds, where we'd order French fries. Then I'd drive us to the lake and Mom would toss the fries to the birds. When we stayed in, my brother Bob would often meet us for lunch at the cafeteria.

I also took Mom to the local movie theater. During the movie, I would glance over at her eating a big box of red licorice. I'd think, "This woman is crazy. But she is so sweet."

When my mother needed me the most, I made sure I was there for her. She had always been there for me when I needed her. She was there when my Hee Haw and TV career ended, and she was there when my husband left me. When I cried on her shoulder, "The best part of my life is over," Mom assured me, "A lot of people get married a second time, and they find happiness they've never known."

Mom was right. During one of my visits in 2005, I told Rosie, "I'm getting remarried." She asked, "Who's walking you down the aisle?" I laughed, "Well, I'm 55 and it's my second marriage, so I hadn't thought about it." She quickly answered, "I'll do it." Then, in another moment of clarity, she continued, "Your dad did it the first time and that didn't work out at all."

My 86-year old Mother Rosie kept her word. She had been in a wheelchair, but on my wedding day...in a gazebo above Lake Arrowhead, California, where our dear friend Karen Prisant would marry us, just before the big moment...Rosie got out of her wheelchair, and walked me down the aisle. By the way, who was my husband Barry's best man? His 90-year old Dad Bernie!

People sometimes ask what happened to all of the beautiful dresses and gowns I wore throughout my career. They especially want to know what happened to the famous pink dress I wore at the

Cannes Film Festival. The answer will probably surprise you...I gave them all away to a bunch of old ladies!

The nursing home where my mother was at, was having a beauty contest for its residents. So I donated all my gowns and dresses, including my Cannes dress to them. My mother came in third place. She was beaten out by a woman who used a walker and an oxygen tank...but she sure had a nice dress! So today, there is probably some 90-year-old woman, wearing one of my fancy evening gowns, and that's totally fine with me.

I want to publicly thank my sister-in-law, Lynn Rowe for the care she gave both my mother and father. She also watched over Dad at the end of his life. Lynn became a hospice nurse, but she always made sure Mom had the very best care possible. Her co-workers truly loved the residents they took care of. They proved that love when all the nurses gave up their raises for the year. They used that money to buy patio furniture, so the older people could go out into the garden and sit in the sunshine.

When I saw that act of kindness, I also wanted to do something for the facility. So, I put on a performance of my play, "Fandance, The Legend of Sally Rand." It turned into a very successful fundraiser for the Bear Valley Community Hospital.

I bought Mom a DVD player, but in her last years, she would only watch two things. One was a DVD of "Gone with the Wind," and the other was my live "A Misty Christmas Show." It was the one that featured her and my daughter in the dance contest. She wanted to watch that video every single day. The nurses would put it on and then walk out of her room, but just when the part with her was about to come on, she would yell, "Come in here and watch this!" Every day. And every day, a nurse would come in and watch Rosie win the dance contest.

As I watched my mother battle Alzheimer's disease, I started keeping a journal. She did some very strange things, but she knew me right up until two weeks before she died. She couldn't remember my name, but she knew I was her daughter. I turned my journal into a little play called, "Forget Me Not."

"Forget Me Not" is a true memoir of my mother's journey with Alzheimer's. Some of it is sad. Some is shocking, and some is very funny. My mother was a hoot until the very end.

I was getting ready to perform my "Blondes Still Have More Fun!" live stage show in New York, when I got a call from Lynn, who said my mom was near death, and they were putting her on morphine. As I started thinking I should cancel my show and fly to California, I received an email from Julie Grandi.

Julie is the wonderful woman who has typed up all of my scripts and projects I've written over the years. To make sure I stayed in New York, Mom had Julie take a photo of her as she held a postcard that promoted my concert. Mom was giving a thumbs up, to make sure I knew that "the show must go on."

Mom died in 2013, at the age of 94. She had been in nursing facilities for 11 years. After her death, Mom's nurse, Regina Garrison stayed in touch with me, and each July, she still remembers her birthday on Facebook. What a joy she was.

FROM DUMB BLONDE TO REAL ESTATE MOGUL

Lots of people dream of fame and fortune. I did too. And I actually ended up with a little bit of fame and a surprising amount of fortune…at least at some points in my life. I have taken my bank account on quite a roller coaster ride over the years, as it started at zero, slowly worked its way up, up and up, and then came crashing back down. Then I started the ride all over again. I found that becoming rich and famous was really the easy part. Staying rich and famous was a lot more difficult.

I can honestly say that I never got rich from my TV and movie work. I made $12, 000 in the first year I was on Hee Haw. That's $12, 000 for the entire year! And the TV series "Happy Days" paid me $325 a show. So no, I didn't make my fortune from TV.

But I found another way to make money, and I was very good at it. (No, it's not what you are thinking. Get your mind out of the gutter.) I made my money in real estate!

Early in my career, I noticed that all of my friends, had no money. Even the working actresses, those who were lucky enough to get an acting job, were always broke. That's a sad thing about the acting profession. You could land a great series, but it may only go on for five years and then you never get another acting job again. Ever.

I was living with my boyfriend Robert in 1974, and I told him, "I don't want to have to live week to week, just barely making ends meet." Robert was older than I, and he had more life experience than I did. He said, "You need to try to save your money and buy a little house. You could rent it out, and the house would turn into an investment for the future."

It was great advice. Unfortunately, a short time later, Robert and I had a big fight and he threw me out of his apartment! When I came home to see all my clothes out in the hall, I told myself, "I really need to get my own place."

I started looking for a little house and I found one in Laurel Canyon. It was a two-bedroom, two-bath with tall ceilings and a fireplace. The asking price was $36,000. I was in my second year of Hee Haw and I had saved some money; $4,000.

I went to Great Western Bank to ask for a loan. After filling out a hundred forms, they asked what I could offer as collateral. I told them the only thing I had was my Hee Haw contract. I was in my second year with the show, and my contract was for three years. I also gave them Sam Lovullo's name as a reference.

The banker explained that I would need to put a down payment of 20%, and with closing costs, I would need at least $8,000. I told them I only had half of that. But before they asked me to leave, the banker said that he would go ahead and call Sam Lovullo.

When Sam got on the phone, he told them that, yes I did have just one year left on my contract. He also commented, "But I have absolute confidence that we are going to re-sign her. And I would be willing to advance all of her residuals for the reruns of Hee Haw for next year."

Thanks to Sam, I was approved for my home loan. After all the papers were signed, the banker told me I was the youngest single woman to ever get a mortgage from Great Western. The first person I called to tell about my new house was Marianne Gordon Rogers. Marianne was so happy for me, saying, "Two years ago, you were the ditzy girl borrowing money from me to buy lunch. Now you are buying your own home!" She was so proud of me.

As most first-time buyers find out, getting the loan is the easy part. But making the monthly payments on time is the big challenge. My mortgage with taxes and insurance was $290 a month. I worried how I was going to make that money each month.

To help pay the bills, I invited a friend from high school, Cyndee Rabourn, to come live with me. Cyndee had made costumes for all our school plays. Cyndee was working at a local department store and said she would love to live with me. I always enjoyed having a roommate. I went from being home with my parents and siblings to living with a roommate at the Hollywood Studio. Then I shared an apartment with my boyfriend and now that I was in my own home, I also took on a roommate. Today, I joke that I was never home alone until I got married!

Cyndee and I shared our house for two years, until she moved out to marry Michael Milligan. And then I found another person to share the rent in an unlikely place…a broom closet.

At the Actor's Workshop, I found out that a nice man named Bleu McKenzie was actually living in a broom closet! I don't know how he did it. I approached him and asked, "Bleu, how would you like to sleep in a real bed and have your own bathroom?" I explained that his room would be separate from my part of the house. The next day, Bleu moved in. He eventually worked as my security and came to my rescue a number of times.

In early 1976, my accountant called and said, "Misty, with your acting career really taking off, your financial circumstances have changed a lot. You're making a lot more money than you did before, especially after your Playboy pictorial. You're single and you need deductions. If not, the government is going to take 60% of your income."

I asked him what I should do, and he said, "You need a bigger house. You need to upgrade to a much more expensive home." So, I put my little home up for sale, and it sold the first day it was on the market. Two years after I bought it for $36,000, I sold it for $80,000.

I started looking for a new house and my real estate agent Jeanie said I should move to Beverly Hills. I told her I couldn't afford to live in Beverly Hills. But she said she lived by the motto of "buying the worst house in the best area." The next day, she called and said, "I've found your home in Beverly Hills. It's the worst one around!"

It was a three-story Spanish, built in 1928. Back in the day, it had been a speakeasy, and get ready for it…it was hanging off the side of a cliff! It was so run down, with weeds that were three feet tall in the yard. When I opened the door, the doorknob fell off in my hand. When I looked at the big holes that were in the walls, I told my realtor, "Yes, I am sure this is the very worst house in Beverly Hills. I guess I will take it."

I paid $119,000 for the home that was just a mile from Sunset Boulevard. The great actress Carol Channing lived just down the road. Bleu McKenzie, my security guard, also made the move to Beverly Hills with me. He had his own bedroom and bath and a separate entrance.

Bleu enjoyed sharing the home, and I was so thankful he was around, especially the day I came face to face with my first stalker. I noticed a man standing outside, looking at my house. I didn't think much about it, but the next day, the man rang the doorbell. When I came to the door, he asked if he could go to the studio with me. I quickly asked him to leave and went to Bleu's part of the house to tell him about the unsettling incident.

The next day, I looked out the window and saw the man behind a bush in my yard. I yelled for Bleu, and he grabbed my shotgun. Bleu calmly stepped out on the front step. He stood there for a couple minutes, with the gun at his side, then came back in. When my stalker found out that a large man, who brandished a shotgun also lived here, I never saw him again.

When my Grandpa Johnson turned 80 years old, my Father went on a tirade and cut his telephone wires. Then he took Grandpa's furniture and threw it into the street. Mom called me in hysterics and I said, "Bring Grandpa to me." He had been so good to me when I was a little girl, and I was happy to share my home with him.

But there was one problem. I didn't have enough room for three people, so that would mean Bleu had to move out. I felt so bad when I told Bleu, and I felt even worse when he quietly said, "It's OK, Miss Misty, I understand. And I want to thank you for giving me my first home."

I just melted. I thought a moment and asked, "Bleu, would you mind sleeping in the garage? I'll fix it up for you, and there's a half bath you can use." He said, "I slept in the closet at the Actor's Workshop, so the garage will be more than enough."

I went to the bank and I got a line of credit so I could turn the garage into a home. It turned into a great move for all of us. I was traveling all the time and was rarely home. Bleu continued to protect my place and since Grandpa was old and didn't have a car, Bleu would watch over him and drive him anywhere he needed to go.

We really became a family. We would cook together, and he loved burritos. He would eat them every day. Grandpa would do the dishes, and he'd prune our roses and watch the dogs while I was away.

One day, I invited Marianne Rogers over for dinner. Grandpa was cooking mashed potatoes, as he looked out the window. He suddenly asked, "Did someone die?" I looked out and said, "That's Marianne's limo." Grandpa asked, "There's just one person in a car that long?"

In March of 1980, Grandpa and I watched an episode of "Laverne and Shirley" together. Afterwards I said, "I'm tired, grandpa, I'm going to bed. I love you." He said, "I love you, too, dear." And he passed in the middle of the night. It broke my heart.

But I always feel that Grandpa is watching over me. When I was working at Universal Studios, on my lunch hour, I would run by Taco Bell, and then go eat my lunch at the cemetery where Grandpa was buried. Instead of flowers, I always left a burrito at his grave.

I paid $119,000 for the house where I lived with Grandpa and Bleu. Fifteen years later, I sold that house for almost one million dollars! Today, it is worth $4.5 million.

I invested that money into properties with my new husband. We bought a condo for $250,000 and put $400,000 toward a huge home. I didn't mind using all the money I had made on my own before our marriage. I felt I was investing in our future, and in our marital property. That sounded good at the time…until we divorced, and my husband said he was entitled to half of everything.

I have now bought and sold 10 homes in my lifetime. Buying and selling houses seemed to come natural to me. Both my brothers were contractors. My brother Eddie, who used to torment me as a child, was a big help to me when I started buying houses.

I had a home in Greenwich, Connecticut and then I had one up in the mountains at Big Bear Lake. Every house I ever bought and sold on my own, I made money on. And every home I bought and sold with my ex-husband, we lost money on. It's really all about timing, and like Kenny Rogers always sang, "You've got to know when to hold them, know when to fold them. Know when to walk away…"

PATSY

My husband was gone. Our divorce was final. I had given up my TV and movie career for our marriage, and now it was all gone. All the excitement, fame and fortune I had enjoyed for the last two decades were now just a memory, as I lived with my two-year old daughter in Connecticut. Dreama was the one bright spot in my life, and I wasn't about to give up custody of her, even if we didn't have any money. In order to pay our bills, I had to sell everything I owned.

My friend Joan Kovats, the licensing director for the stage musical "Always…Patsy Cline" came to visit me. When she saw that my house was up for sale and I didn't have anything on my acting horizon, she announced, "This cannot be! You need to be working. I want you to audition for "Always…Patsy Cline."

"Always…Patsy Cline" is a two woman, 6-piece band production, that tells the story of the friendship between the country music legend and one of her fans, Louise Seger.

Joan asked me to fly out to Denver, Colorado to see the production at a performing arts center. She wanted me to meet the creator of the show and audition for the part of Louise. She also told me they couldn't pay for my airfare or my hotel room, so I would have to foot the entire bill myself. But she was very confident that if I went, I would get the part, and she even agreed to watch my baby while I was gone. I looked at Joan and dejectedly said, "I don't even own a suitcase." She walked across the room and dumped all the clothes from her own suitcase, and said, "Take mine. Just get on that plane."

I made the very long flight from Connecticut to Colorado and auditioned for the man who created the show, Ted Swindley. As Joan had predicted, Ted offered me the role, saying, "Misty, you are a hoot! We need to work together." It was a decision that would restart my career.

My first performance in "Always...Patsy Cline" was at the Tony Orlando "Yellow Ribbon" Theater in Branson, Missouri. Kay Crowe played Patsy, I played Louise. I was quite nervous when I found out that the real Louise Seger was coming to my opening night, along with Patsy's husband Charlie Dick.

Ted Swindley wanted me to wear a wig for my role and I went out to a store in Branson and paid $15.00 for one. It had a big, green bow in the back. I knew nothing about wigs, and I bought one that was a little too small. At showtime, I just put it on, with no skull cap and no pins to attach it to my own hair.

During the show, there's a scene where I direct the band, and the more they play, the more animated and excited I get. I was jumping and dancing on top of the bandstand, and when I threw my head back, my wig went flying through the air. It landed on the ground, and I ran and picked up the wig and ran off the stage. The audience was just roaring with laughter.

There was no mirror at the side of the stage, so I just slapped the wig back on my head and ran back out to the bandstand. As soon as the drummer saw me, his eyes widened and he whispered, "Your wig is on backwards." My big, green bow was in the front, and it was obvious to everyone (but me) that it was on wrong.

Louise Seger, who I was playing, got up in the middle of the show, and yelled, "I wouldn't wear that wig to an outhouse!" The crowd continued to laugh, as Louise stormed out of the theater. She was so upset that she spent the rest of the performance, smoking cigarettes in the lobby.

The next day, Patsy's husband, Charlie Dick called me. He said, "Misty, you know the Patsy estate has to approve all the performers, and I'd like to take you to dinner before I tell you what I have to say." I was feeling pretty low when we met, but then he surprised me with, "Misty, you are as funny as you ever were on "Hee Haw," and you brought tears to my eyes with your speech at the end of the show. You are going to be just fine."

I was so glad to have Charlie's blessing. But Louise Seger was a different story. She still hated me. But Charlie talked her into going back to see me one more time. Before my second performance, I purchased a better wig, and made sure it was securely fastened to my head.

During the show, there's a moment when I go out into the audience and dance with someone. When I saw Louise on the aisle of the second row, I held my hand out to her and asked her to dance. She thought a moment and said, "Well, why not…but I lead." From that moment on, we were great friends.

Anytime she could, Louise, would come to the show, and not only would she be in the audience, but afterward, she joined me to meet fans and take photos and sign autographs. Our audiences loved being able to meet "both Louises." When we couldn't be together in person, we exchanged letters. In one, Louise wrote that she never liked it when other actresses portrayed her as "frumpy." She had been a beauty queen in her youth and when I joined the production, she liked the idea of a "Hee Haw Honey" playing her.

Since my first, horrible opening night, can you believe that I've been in more than 1,000 "Always…Patsy Cline" performances?

Over that time, I've worked with more than ten different "Patsys," but Cindy Summers portrayed Patsy in most of those shows.

Cindy is an amazing singer, and when we brought the show to the Downtown Cabaret Theatre in Bridgeport, Connecticut, we broke their 20-year box office record. One of the many people who saw us there was a man named Barry Singer. He got there ten minutes late and didn't get a program. He didn't know who the girl on stage was (me), but he knew that anyone with a huge bee-hive hairdo and mermaid stretch-pants, who could hold the audience in the palm of her hand, must be someone special. I didn't meet Barry that night, but I would very soon. Little did he know when he came to the theater that night, that he would one day have his very own chapter in this book!

After my first 100 performances, the general manager of the Civic Light Opera in California called and said they wanted to book the show, and he also wanted me to be the director. I told him I would check with Ted Swindley, and he said he would begin teaching me how to direct. He gave me a crash course and I learned more than 250 lighting cues in just a short time.

I joined the SDC, which stands for Stage, Directors and Choreographers Society, and became a professional director. My first show as an official SDC director was at the Surflight Theatre in Beach Haven, New Jersey. I found that theater when I volunteered to go with my daughter's class on a field trip to see a play.

My husband and I went back to the theater and when we asked for the general manager, I was surprised to find out it was the man who had been Joe Namath's understudy when Joe and I did our tour with "Lil' Abner." Steven Steiner was so excited to see me again. He'd gone on to have a wonderful career, that included some shows on Broadway. Steve agreed to hire me under my first SDC contract.

From there, my directing career really took off. I directed and starred in "Always...Patsy Cline" at the 2,200 seat Tropicana Showroom in Atlantic City. I also directed "The Ultimate Doo-Wop Christmas Show," that featured some of the all-time great Doo-Wop singers. That turned out so well that I was offered a job directing a show in Las Vegas called "Forever Doo-Wop.

"Forever Doo-Wop" had the most incredible singers, and my husband had worked with a lot of them when he had a show at the Sahara that ran for nine years. It featured an all-black cast, four male and three female. We did have a white DJ, but I wondered what their reaction would be when the whitest, blonde haired girl in the world walked in to tell them how they should Doo-Wop.

It was almost the reverse of "Hee Haw," which had an all-white cast with an occasional black guest artist, but now I was the minority. When the owner of the show introduced me to the cast, any fears I might have had quickly vanished, as the group said, "Misty, we always pray before we rehearse. Would you pray with us?" I joined their circle and we all held hands, and I was overjoyed as I listened to the most sincere prayer I had ever heard, as Early Clover gave thanks for the work they had been offered and for the chance to entertain the people who would come to the show.

I explained that I wasn't there to change any of their singing and dancing, but my main job was to pace the show and light everyone so they would look better than they ever had. I also added some humor to the show as I directed them as they did some old radio jingles, including one for "A-Jax, the foaming cleanser." Those became one of the highlights of the show. That show ran until the Riviera Hotel closed.

I really fell in love with directing. I loved using the lights to make the performers look their very best. It's a lot of fun to get to know the talents of other actors and singers and then use those talents so that they are at their very best.

When I wasn't directing, I continued to appear in productions such as "Pump Boys and Dinettes." Of course, I had the role of the waitress Rhetta Cup, who was known for filling her double cups…her coffee cups! During the song "Tips," I went out into the audience and collected tips, and we gave that money to "Save the Children."

Speaking of full cups…when "Pump Boys and Dinettes" played in Wisconsin, my Auntie Gert came to see me. Aunt Gert was my mother's older sister, and she was one of my very favorite relatives. She had a 40-inch bust and never wore a bra. All my guy friends used to love to hug her. She told me, "The last time I wore a bra was 1950. I came home and took it off and never wore another one."

I did a three-person play called "Groucho – A Life in Review." Gabe Kaplan, who was known for the hit TV series, "Welcome Back Kotter," was the world's biggest Groucho Marx fan, and he did an amazing impression of Groucho. I was the one woman in the play, and I had to play many different characters, with different outfits and accents. That production ran a long time at the Sid Caesar Dinner Theater.

I was in an Off-Broadway production at The Tribeca Playhouse in New York. They were looking for a woman who had a southern accent and liked to talk. Yeah, I got that with no trouble.

I was offered my own show at The Metropolitan Room in New York City. I wrote it all and it was based on my life and was called "Blondes Still Have More Fun." They showed pictures from my career on the big screen behind me, as I told many funny stories, and a few poignant ones about my life. I had a four-piece band and Cindy Summers was also part of that. I rehearsed that show while I was directing a different Patsy Cline production called "A Closer Walk With Patsy Cline."

"Fandance, the Legend of Sally Rand," was a production I wrote, directed and starred in. It told the story of how my mother met the burlesque legend. Barbie Benton came to see "Fandance" when we played at the Performing Arts Center in Big Bear Lake, California. She came from her home in Aspen, Colorado.

In addition to my TV and movie career, I've also done over 3,000 stage performances. I can tell you where the best theater and concert venues are across the country. One of my very favorite places to play is The Historic Savannah Theatre in Savannah, Georgia. To say that its historic is almost an understatement. It first opened in 1818. Legends including W.C. Fields and Oscar Wilde played the Savannah, and even baseball great Ty Cobb took part in a rare stage performance there in 1911.

My 1,000th performance of "Always...Patsy Cline," came at the Main Street Theater on Hilton Head Island. Uncle Chuck, my favorite uncle, lived on Hilton Head, and I was able to spend a month with him while I did the show night after night with my new Patsy, Sara Katherine Wheatly.

Bobby Hamilton was my musical director, and his wife Sara had a beautiful voice. We all shared a house for our month on the Island. When Sara found out I was getting close to my 1,000th show, she made sure we celebrated in style. They surprised me at my curtain call, with flowers, a huge cake, and letters from my dear friend Joan Kovats and from Ted Swindley, who created the show. When I read the words they wrote to me, I just cried and cried.

I've talked a lot about Joan Kovats and how important she has been in my career and my life. Joan's insisting that I fly across the country to audition for "Always...Patsy Cline," was a move that would eventually lead me to meeting the man who would become my husband. So, I have a lot to thank her for, besides all the productions she booked me in over the last 35 years.

I thought it might be fun to ask Joan to share a few of her memories of our time together.

"The first time I met Misty, I heard that unique voice of hers, and I immediately started thinking about the productions I could book her in. The first one I got for her was Damn Yankees in April of 1983. She was such a pro, and everyone who worked with her just loved her.

We started spending so much time together, that our working relationship soon became a true friendship, and that eventually became more like a sisterhood. I consider her more like a sister than a friend. We both had brothers, but neither of us had a sister, so we became soul sisters.

We have gone through so much of our lives together, good times and bad times. We were there for each other when we both went through divorces, when we both suffered miscarriages, and when we celebrated the births of our children. Misty is the Godmother of my son Erik, and she would babysit him and I would babysit her daughter Dreama.

My dad loved Hee Haw and his favorite person on the show was Misty. I introduced him to her, and they became best friends. When Misty had her miscarriage in New York City, Dad took her to the hospital. When she did her play Just Another Blonde, Dad ran the concession stand and sold lemonade and cookies.

Dad ended up running Misty's fan club and he also did repair work around her house. But they became so close, that he would go over to fix something, and they would end up playing Scrabble all afternoon. He adored her, and she adored him, and their deep friendship made the last ten years of my dad's life the happiest he had ever been. I thank Misty for giving him that.

Misty is so sensitive and tender. She has no airs about her, and she does not act like a celebrity in any way. She is kind to her fans and to anyone she meets. Misty is like a little angel here on earth.

I know if I need anything, Misty is just a phone call away. She is a loyal friend, and is a very, very rare human being. The first time I met her, there was just something magical about her. I felt that so much that I gave her the name Magical Misty. And she still has that same magic today. She has such a light about her. You don't come across people like her very often."

- Joan Kovats

A GUY NAMED BARRY

I had gone through a terrible divorce. I was now a single mom. Our house was being sold and I had no idea where we'd be living. I was sinking into a deep depression.

My mother offered me her advice, "Misty, please try to remember that many people get married for a second time and they live happily ever after."

It turns out that Mom was right. The second time was indeed the charm. I met a wonderful man named Barry more than two decades ago, and we are living happily ever after.

I met Barry in a Casino in Atlantic City. But neither of us was gambling. And we probably wouldn't have ended up together if Grand Ole Opry star Jeannie Seely hadn't forgot her lines.

For years, I had appeared in the musical "Always…Patsy Cline." But I wanted to start directing the production, and the show's creator Ted Swindley, said he would mentor me. He said I should come sit with him in the director's booth when they did the production at the

Claridge Casino. I spent four days learning from Ted and I also met the producer of the show, Barry Singer.

Jeannie Seely was playing the role of Louise, which I usually did. Ted thought that Jeannie needed a blonde wig, and I volunteered to go get one. Barry Singer said he would come along so he could pay for it. We visited on the way, but mainly just talked about the production and everything that we needed to do to get ready.

The opening night was a very cold January evening. But even with the cold, it still sold out. As the show began, everything ran smoothly. I could tell Jeannie was at home on the stage. But I also knew she had never had to memorize lines like she had to for this. She had over 700 lines to learn, and sure enough, halfway through it, she "went up." When an actor on stage forgets where they are in a play, we say they "went up." And Jeannie went way up.

Since this was a non-equity production, there was no one "on book" to help her. 'On book' is someone who stands at the side of the stage or in the front row and they always have a script they are following, so they can throw out the next line if an actor forgets one. There was no one to throw out any lines to Jeannie.

She started to cry. She totally stopped and started apologizing to the audience. She said, "I am so sorry, but I have no idea where I am in this."

Joan Kovats, the licensing agent for the show, yelled, "Misty! Go save her!" I crept up to the stage and started loudly whispering the next line to Jeannie. She looked down at me and yelled, "What?!"

Once she got that line, Jeannie took off and never missed another one all night. At the end of the evening, the crowd gave her a standing ovation. As the happy audience filed out, Barry Singer

Modeling Marilyn's
Seven Year Itch
Dress.

Visiting Marilyn's star on the
Hollywood Walk of Fame.

Oh, this ol' thing. It's just something I threw on.

As I look back at these,
I guess I did look quite
a bit like Marilyn.

I can't read a
word of it, but
I made the
cover!

Posing for Chris Barham from the London Daily Mail newspaper.

The London press even followed me into my bathtub!
Photo by Victor Blackman, Daily Express

London premiere for Goodbye, Norma Jean, 1976

I guess you could say that all eyes were on me!

Meeting Elton John, Sept. 1976.

Giving Elton John a rose. Photo by Dego Hoffman.

MISTY ROWE SERA-T-ELLE LA NOUVELLE MARILYN MONROE?

A French magazine asks, "Will she be the new Marilyn Monroe?"

My innocent
girl look.

Making the cover of a
TV magazine with Buck
and Gunilla.

With Barbie, doing our
Gossipy Girls skit.

Sammy Davis Jr. visits the Kornfield, 1981

Hee Haw's makeup person, Elizabeth Linneman.
She made us all look beautiful.

Anson Williams is about
to get a Banana Split.

MISTY ROWE
ON
"HAPPY DAYS"
TONIGHT 8:00 p.m. Channel 7

MISTY IS WINDY
(ALL FALL ON "HAPPY DAYS")

Trade ad promoting my role
on Happy Days.

Working with
Ron Howard and
Donny Most.

The Fonz gives Wendy a Christmas gift.

Henry Winkler
handwrote this
poem on the back
of one of his
script pages.

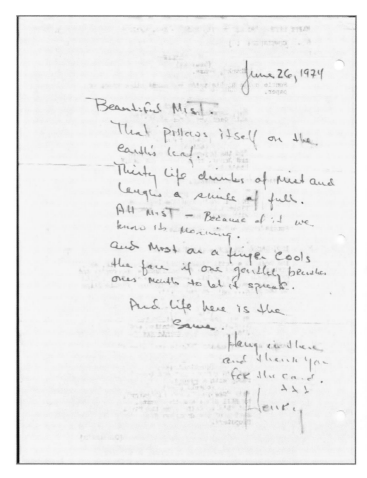

With Marianne and
Kenny Rogers.

Lulu Roman gets up close with Kenny Rogers during a break.

Some of my dearest friends. Dave Rowland, Marianne and Kenny Rogers.

Dave Rowland holds a BR-549 sign as he stands in front of his Elvis car that I wrecked.

Dave Rowland
was the only
country star I
ever dated.

With Elton John and Dave Rowland during a party at Elton's home.

My dear friend
Michael Hewitson,
Sir Elton John's
valet. In 1977 and
in 2000.

Riding the Hee Haw float in the Rose Parade. Buck Owens is on the front, while all the Hee Haw Honeys wave to the crowd.

MISTY ROWE

My poster that sold over one million copies.

Photo by Buddy Rosenberg

Cover of TV
Chronilog
magazine.

June 16-22, 1985

'Hee Haw's'
Misty Rowe
(See Pages 6-7)

Goober says Hey!
With George
Lindsey.

The cast of When Things Were Rotten.

Misty Rowe
As Maid Marian and
Mel Brooks demolish a legend in 'When Things Were Rotten'

Comedy great
Mel Brooks
always made me
laugh.

As Maid Marian to Dick Gautier's Robin Hood.

With Ron Rifkin as I get married during my favorite
episode of When Things Were Rotten.

I was one of an all-star cast in SST Death Flight.

With Michelle Phillips and Robert Sacchi in The Man With Bogart's Face.

Playing Dutchess in The Man with Bogart's Face.

The Hee Haw Honeys cast photo. Misty, Kenny Price, Gailard Sartain, Lulu Roman and Kathie Lee Johnson.

Kathie Lee Johnson, Gailard Sartain and Misty.

Celebrating my birthday on the set of Hee Haw Honeys. (L-R) Lulu Roman, Sam Lovullo, Director Bob Boatman and writer Barry Adelman.

Living legend Loretta Lynn sings on our Hee Haw Honeys show.

Conway Twitty visits Hee Haw Honeys.

With Barbara Mandrell

3 Minnies. Misty, June Carter Cash, Minnie Pearl on a Johnny Cash TV special.

Howdy! With the legendary Minnie Pearl.

Riding in Goliath as I wave to the truck pull crowd.

Behind the wheel
of a monster truck
in Dayton, Ohio.
Photo by Harry
Dunn

Making a few laps before the Indianapolis 500.

With Gunilla Hutton at the bridal shower she threw for me.

A photo by the one and only Harry Langdon.

With Hee Haw hunk Jeff Smith.

My security guard Bleu McKenzie and my film acting couch Estelle Harman

This was the 2nd choice for my poster, but they chose my cut-off jeans inst[e

She has lived up to her name...Dreama.

My mother attends A Misty Christmas. Little did I know she would steal the show!

A Misty Christmas at the Claridge Casino Hotel.

At age 50, I wrote and starred in the stage production A Misty Christmas.

Photo by Paulo Filqueiras

A Misty Christmas. (L-R) Mark Enis, Bryce Bermingham, Misty, Peter Dinklage, Cindy Summers.

A Misty Christmas cast. Peter Dinklage, Bryce Bermingham, Misty,
Cindy Summers, Mark Enis.

With Gabe Kaplan and Bob Ader in *Groucho, a Life in Review.*

My daughter Dreama after seeing one too many Groucho shows!

My daughter wearing the dress I wore to the Cannes Film Festival in 1975.

Misty at 56.

Misty Rov

On the road again with Willie Nelson.

I loved Roy Clark so much!

With my dear
friend Marianne
Gordon Rogers.

With Phyllis George and Marianne's decorator Rachel. Phyllis passed
away as I was writing this book.

Trying to help others by sharing our stories.
My friends from the griefHaven group.

My brother taking Dad for a ride in the super-charged dune buggy Bob built.

My dad and sister
in-law Lynn.

With Dad after his stroke.

With Ted Swindley, the creator of Always...Patsy Cline.

With Kay Crowe (my first Patsy) and Patsy's husband Charlie Dick.

My band for Blondes Still Have More Fun. Left to right, Zach Jones, Michael Sansonia, Misty, Cindy Summers, Steve Steiner and Fooch Fishetti. Photo by Chuck LaPadula

The Dynamic Duo. Misty as Louise and Cindy Summers as Patsy Cline.

On stage with
Cindy Summers,
1999.

Giving it everything
I've got with Tori
Lynn Palazola.

Curtain call after my 1, 000 performance of Always...Patsy Cline.

Ted Swindley, the man who taught me how to be a professional director.

Our wedding day. (L-R) Barry's dad Bernie, Barry, Rosie, Misty, Dreama

My mother walks me down the aisle for my second (and last) wedding!

My best friend Mary Jo Thatcher, Minister Karen Prisant-Ellis , Misty,
Hee Haw designer Faye Sloan.

Barry would do anything
to entertain my daughter!

One of my favorite photos of Barry and Dreama.

Barry poses for the last photo with the 3 Dames. Misty, Rosie, Dreama.

At the Salute to the Kornfield reunion. (L-R) Lulu Roman, Barbie Benton, Misty, Gunilla Hutton.

With Dreama on the night she won the title of
Princess of Big Bear Lake.

Visiting the original Kornfield, now at the Country Music Hall of Fame, with Danny Forbes and Barbie Benton.

The Kornfield Friends appear on the Mike Huckabee Show. (L-R) Buck Trent Misty, Gov. Mike Huckabee, Lulu Roman, Jana Jae.
Photo by Kris Rae-Huckabee Show.

My husband Barry (bottom right) joins the cast of A Hee Haw Honey Reunion including Victoria Hallman, Lulu Roman and Bobby and Sara Hamilton. Photo by Ali Jansen

Directing the cast of Forever Doo Wop in Las Vegas. Photo by Stephen Thorburn

With Dolly Parton and Hee Haw wardrobe designer Faye Sloan.

Celebrating my 60th birthday with Noel and Katherine Blanc.

Together again, with
Donny Most.

Introducing my dear friend Sandi Bria to Donny Most.

Celebrating Christmas with Dreama, 2019.

With a guy named Barry.

came up to me saying, "Thank you so much for giving her that line. You totally saved the show."

Then Barry "made his move" as he said, "I want to thank you. Can I take you to dinner? I know a great Italian place." I answered, "Sure, but since it's so cold, I'll need to run up to my room and get my coat." While I did that, Barry ran outside and saw a limousine running in front of the casino. Barry asked the driver to take us to a restaurant that was a couple miles away. The driver said, "I'm sorry, I can't. This is a private limo and I'm waiting on someone." Barry said, "I'll give you $20 if you just run us there. It's just two miles away." The driver said "Ok, but we need to go now."

I came down, wearing my coat and I asked Barry, "Don't you need a coat?" He said, "No, I'll be fine," and we jumped into the back of "our" limo. On the way, I was thinking, "Wow, this Barry is a big, fancy producer. He has nice, warm car and everything."

When we got to the restaurant, (which was a lot farther than two miles) as soon as we got out and started walking in, the limo driver sped away. I saw Barry's eyes widen as he reached for the door handle and saw a sign that read 'Closed.' I said, "Oh, that's Ok, we can go somewhere else," as I turned around to walk back to our car. Our car that was long gone.

I glanced around and realized that we were in a bad part of Atlantic City at 11:00 at night. Today, we would just use our cell phone and call an Uber to come get us. But this was 20 years ago, and we didn't have cell phones or Ubers.

Our only option was to walk back to our hotel. As we started our multi-mile trek, I began thinking, "How could this night get any worse?" I would soon find out. It started snowing!

Luckily, I had my coat, leather gloves, and a fur hat. But Barry had nothing. He was wearing slacks, a shirt and cowboy boots. The temperature was 19 degrees, and we were freezing. In an effort to warm up (at least that's what I'll say) Barry started to curse. A lot.

After about a dozen curse words, I started to laugh, and I was soon laughing my head off. Then I asked, "Why did your limo driver leave us?" Barry said, "That wasn't my car. I wanted to impress you, so I borrowed someone else's car."

I gave him one of my gloves to use and we continued our long, winter walk. We finally made it to a café and we went in and warmed up with hot tea and soup. They called us a cab to pick us up and take us back to the hotel. That was our first "date." It sure was one that neither of us will ever forget.

During our soup and tea that night, (after Barry had stopped cussing) I shared with him my dream of producing a Christmas musical. I had always wanted to put on a big stage extravaganza. He laughed when I told him the name I had already chosen for it -'A Misty Christmas, Finally a Fruitcake You'll Like,' starring Misty Rowe and her chestnuts. Barry asked, "What are your chestnuts?" I shot back, "They're my jokes! They can also be the other singers and dancers who are in the show."

A short time later, Barry agreed to come to Connecticut where my manager and I officially presented him with the Christmas show idea. Barry thought the show would work and he prepared to pitch the idea to the entertainment director of the Claridge Casino, where he had done "Always…Patsy Cline." I gave him boxes and boxes of videos of my TV and movie appearances, and he edited it all down to a 10-minute promotional tape. When he played it for the entertainment bookers, they said, "Oh yes, we grew up with Misty. We love her! Of course, she can have her own show."

Barry called and said, "Get your sexy Santa suit cleaned. Your dream of a Christmas extravaganza is coming true." It turned out to be one of the greatest productions that I ever did. I worked very hard preparing for "A Misty Christmas.' I took aerobics to get in the best shape of my life, and I hired my line dance teacher Pam as the choreographer. She taught me and the other actors how to dance around the stage while we sang, without running out of breath.

My friend Faye Sloan, who did all the wardrobe for Hee Haw, came in and handmade the most beautiful outfits for our musical. We had a live four-piece band and I also featured Cindy Summers, who I worked with on "Always...Patsy Cline." Cindy was, by far, the best voice on our stage.

During our auditions, a young man named Peter Dinklage tried out to be one of my "chestnuts." Peter had holes in his sweater, and was totally unknown at the time. Peter was a dwarf, but his personality was bigger than anyone's. My "Misty Christmas" was one of his first acting jobs, and then he went on to become very famous as a multi-Emmy winning star of "Game of Thrones."

I taught Peter to tap dance and I knew he was headed places when he asked if he could have a few free tickets to the show. He said he was going to give them to a director who wanted to see him perform. That director ended up hiring Peter for one of his very first movies.

After two weeks of rehearsals, we pulled into the casino parking lot, I saw a picture of me wearing a Santa hat-3 stories high on the side of the casino/hotel. The same picture was featured on billboards around Atlantic City. Inside the casino, every employee was wearing a button with my photo on it.

I wrote the entire production and came up with a very unique show opening. It started quite elegantly, but ended with me getting stuck inside a giant 10-foot tall Christmas tree ornament. I was eventually able to crash my way out of the ornament. At least that was the plan.

The ornament frame was made of wood and it was covered with white butcher paper, that I would run through, like high school football players do when they run out on the field. Since Barry was the producer of the show, and since Barry always likes to watch the financial bottom line, (he doesn't like to spend money!) he wouldn't let us practice me crashing through the butcher paper. My first time coming through the paper would be on opening night. We should have practiced.

When the time came for me to burst through the paper ornament, I took a few steps back so I could run through and when I hit the paper, the only part of me that made it through was one leg! The audience could see my high heel shoe and leg sticking there. I finally took my arms and tore the rest of the paper away. When I finally got out, I got the biggest laugh of my life.

The next day, I didn't want to look at the reviews in the paper. I had poured my heart and soul into this production and when something has your own name in the title, negative reviews can be devastating. I was especially worried after the opening number ornament fiasco. But when we opened the newspaper, the headline was, "Misty Christmas brightens holidays and Atlantic City is better for it." We received wonderful reviews for the show, and it ran for five weeks.

"A Misty Christmas" wasn't a religious show. It had corny jokes with fun music and skits, but Barry thought it needed a poignant song near the end. We chose one written by my Hee Haw Honey buddy Linda Thompson-Jenner, called "My Grown-Up Christmas List." Before I sang it, I shared some memories of some of the Christmas' I had when I was a little girl.

As we got to know each other, Barry and I started to spend more time together. But since he lived in New Jersey and I was in Connecticut, that time was very limited.

Barry had a daughter named Kimberly, and a son named Todd, from a previous marriage. When children are involved, dating again is much different than it once was. You don't want to bring someone into your children's life and then have them leave when you break up.

Just after my divorce, Dreama really missed her dad, and she wanted me to get re-married as soon as possible. If the UPS man knocked on our door, Dreama would ask him, "Would you like to marry my mommy?" She asked the same question to one of my first dates, and for some reason, he never called for a second one!

But I knew Barry was someone special before I introduced him to my daughter. Dreama loves her father, but she was instantly drawn to Barry. Barry had two grandchildren, Tori and Jade, who were Dreama's age, so he knew children. From the first day they met, Barry was very tender and patient with her. Dreama would ask him to put one of my wigs on and he would do it. They put on puppet shows together and she'd make him play a king, complete with our quilt tied around him and a toy crown on his head. Dreama just adored him.

Barry has been good to my daughter. He was also very good to my mother. And I knew he must have had true love for me when he volunteered to take a very long and miserable trip.

When I met Barry, my mother was living with me, and when she got Alzheimer's, I moved her back home to California. I didn't know how I was going to get my 14-year-old dog Max across the country, because the vet said he was too old to fly. Max had been with me from the time I lived in California, through a move to Connecticut and another move to New Jersey.

I wasn't about to move back to California without Max, so Barry volunteered to drive him 3,000 miles in my Jeep, all the way from Atlantic City, New Jersey, to Big Bear Lake, California. That would have been a big enough challenge. But Max never liked to be alone, so the first night Barry stopped at a hotel, he put Max in the room while he went out for supper. When he came back, the manager had left a note, requesting that he leave the premises immediately, because the dog hadn't stopped barking and was disturbing all the other guests.

So, for the next 2,500 miles, he could only eat at drive-thrus so he could stay in the car with Max. He also had my daughter's little dog, "Tinker Bell", but she was not much trouble for him. But when a man does something like that for you, you have no doubt that he truly loves you.

I went with Barry for 6 years before I married him. We have now been married over 14 years. In that time, we have never had a fight and we have never cheated on each other. Barry also listens when I talk, and I like to talk a lot! After 20 years, many husbands tune out their wives, but he is always there, looking into my eyes, listening to what I have to say.

During most of our marriage, Barry has been a theatrical producer, helping put on shows like "Forty Second Street" and "Footloose." Of course, he did my show "Always...Patsy Cline," and he also produced a huge show called "Forever Motown." It seemed that he was always busy working somewhere and I was always on the road in another state, working on a different project.

But all of that came to a stop in the spring of 2020. When the Corona virus hit, all the theaters across the country closed down. Our very busy life came to a very abrupt stop, (like millions of other people's lives did).

We live on a 900 acre island and our state and our little community issued 'Stay at home' orders and we spent most of the year in the house. We spent that time reading lots of books and going on walks together. Since we couldn't go out to eat, Barry started cooking more. He makes fabulous roast chicken and the best pancakes I've ever eaten. He was a cook in the Army, and he used to make 500 pancakes every morning.

We also kept ourselves busy working on this book. Our house was a total mess as I brought in boxes of memorabilia that had been in storage in our shed. We went through scrapbooks and photo albums, most that Barry had never even seen.

When we were married, we vowed "for richer and for poorer." I believe I became richer because Barry's family always surrounded me with love. His mother Ruthie called me her daughter, even before we were married. His brother David is married to Diana Venegas, who had been Miss Latin America. Diana is elegant and was once a dress designer for Dolly Parton, Tanya Tucker and Priscilla Presley.

Diana calls me her sister and has let me into her children's lives. I love Nicholas and Czarina, and I love her daughter Lysandra, who calls me "Auntie Misty." Two new additions have recently been added to our family joy, Jacob (Barry's grandson) and Venice Rose (our great niece.)

I was originally going to give this chapter a different name. But instead, I will end the chapter with it. It sums up how I see the last 20 years of my life. I have been…. Blessed by Barry.

THE CORN KEEPS ON GROWING

After Hee Haw, Roy Clark went on to become one of the "Kings of Branson." Roy opened his own theater in Branson, Missouri and made millions. I attended one of his shows there, and in the middle of his performance, he stopped the concert and said, "There is a woman here tonight who helped make our Kornfield famous." He asked me to stand up and we visited backstage after his concert.

In the spring of 2007, I was surprised to receive a call from Sam Lovullo. I hadn't seen Sam since I had filed the lawsuit against him. But he said he had forgiven me and forgotten any troubles we had. I explained again that I had just been trying to stand up for myself and it was never anything personal against him. I knew that he completely understood when he asked, "Misty, do you remember when they said Hee Haw wouldn't last? Well, 50 years later, we are getting the Entertainers Award at the TV Land Awards in Hollywood!"

That year, the TV Land Awards honored the shows "Taxi," "The Brady Bunch," and "Hee Haw." I took my daughter as my guest. Dreama was 15, and we walked the red carpet together. One of the first people I saw there was Christopher Knight, from "The Brady Bunch." I had worked with him on the series "Joe's World." When I saw him in his tuxedo, I yelled, "Christopher!" He ran over and took photos with my daughter and he was so nice.

During the ceremony, Willie Nelson, the Judds and k.d. lang all sang during the tribute to "Hee Haw." As k.d. announced our award, I thought back to her memorable appearance on "Hee Haw." She was new and none of us knew her. To be honest, she was so different that we didn't really know what to think. But when she opened her mouth and started singing, she just blew everyone away. It was incredible. After the taping, she invited all of the Hee Haw Honeys to her concert that night at the Ryman Auditorium. During the show, she dedicated a song to all of us and then sang it while she was lying flat on her back!

I sat next to Roy Clark for the awards, and the Hager Brothers and a lot of the Hee Haw Honeys were also there. We had such a large group and I was surprised when they announced each of us by name and had each one come up on stage to accept our own TV Land Award trophy. I thought, "Wow, this is much better than my "Miss Rigid Tool" award.

From that moment on, I once again had a wonderful relationship with Sam Lovullo. We became closer than we had ever been before. When I would have a new stage production, he would come support me and cheer me on. When he came to see my "Fandance" musical, he took Barry, my mother and me out to dinner afterward. He was so impressed with the show that he said, "If I was younger and had a little more money, I would try to get that production to Broadway."

Sam invited me to dinner at his home and his wife Grace pulled me aside and whispered, "I'm so glad you and Sam are back together, and back on track. When the show let all you girls go, I told him he should quit too, that it was also time for him to leave."

Later that year, I got a call from Sam. He explained that the Pacific Pioneer Broadcasters were going to honor Roy Clark, and he asked if I would come and speak at the award ceremony. When I got there, I visited with Sam, Roy, Barbie Benton, Marianne Rogers, Linda Thompson and Gunilla Hutton. Since Roy and Sam were huge baseball fans, Los Angeles Dodger manager Tommy Lasorda also spoke. After the event, Sam sent me a handwritten letter thanking me for being a part of Roy's tribute. I still have that letter that he signed, "Love you always, Sam."

It was always good to see a few of my Hee Haw family members during those occasional special occasions. But the biggest Hee Haw reunion would come in the fall of 2011.

Larry Black, the producer of the Country's Family Reunion TV shows and the star of "Larry's Country Diner" hosted a "Salute to the Kornfield" TV event that aired over four separate hours on RFD TV. When I got the call, asking me to be a part of the taping in Nashville, I immediately thought of the many prayers I had sent up during my lawsuit against the Gaylord Corporation. I had been told I would never work in Nashville again. I had prayed that would not be true, and now those prayers were being answered. I was being invited back to Music City.

More than 20 of the original Hee Haw cast members came together to pick and grin one more time. A dozen country stars, including Moe Bandy, John Conlee, T. Graham Brown, Johnny Lee and Ricky Skaggs sang and talked about how important the show was to their careers. I had such a wonderful time catching up with my friends Cathy Baker, Lulu Roman, Irlene Mandrell and so many more.

I can't put into words what a magical day that was. I felt like I had stepped back into time when Elizabeth Linneman walked in to do my makeup, just like she did for 19 years on the show. When I saw Gwen Anken Bauer in the mirror, styling my hair once again, I said, "I think I've left Hee Haw and gone into the Twilight Zone."

I hadn't planned to sing on the show, but during a break, Charlie McCoy, who had been Hee Haw's musical director, came to me and said, "Misty, I'd like to ask a personal favor. Would you sing the gossipy girls song one more time?" I couldn't say no to Charlie, so we did it.

Before the taping, we had heard that George Lindsey, who had played Goober on Hee Haw, and also "The Andy Griffith Show," had been near death in the hospital. All of us were astounded when the studio door opened, and George slowly walked in. We could see he was very weak and he was using a cane. But he said he wasn't going to miss one last chance to see "his family."

After the taping, as I was packing up in my dressing room, I saw George standing in the doorway. He said, "Misty, I am so glad to see you again. I just want to tell you what an honor it has been to work with you all these years." I ran over and hugged him and said, "Oh, George, the honor was all mine." I was crying as he walked away. George died just after the show was broadcast. It was his last TV appearance.

The "Salute to the Kornfield" was the last time I would get to see a number of my Hee Haw friends, including Gordie Tapp and Don Harron, who played the newscaster Charlie Farquharson. They both passed away less than five years later.

Roy Clark had a very painful back problem and was having trouble walking. As everyone was going into another studio for a cast picture, I took Roy's hand and said, "You want to walk with me?" He smiled his beautiful smile and said, "Yes I do Misty. I sure do." As everyone got in their place for the photo, Roy grabbed my hand and said, "You stay right here, next to me."

After the taping, Hee Haw historian Danny Forbes took Barbie Benton and me on a tour of the Country Music Hall of Fame, where the original Kornfield from the show is on display. Tourist snapped our photo as Barbie and I jumped out of the field and yelled, "Sal...ute!"

In 2015, I wrote a Hee Haw Honey Reunion stage show. Barbie Benton and Victoria Hallman joined me in the show. When I first called Barbie, I told her, "We don't have much of a budget. How much would you need to be paid?" She laughed, "I'll tell you right now that you can't afford me. But I'll do it anyway!" We put on the Hee Haw Honey Reunion at the Performing Arts Center at Big Bear Lake as a fundraiser for the nursing facility where my mother was. Then we had a performance in Palm Desert, California.

I was so happy when I found out that Sam Lovullo had brought his family to the show, and he enjoyed it so much. Sam took us to breakfast the next day and said, "That show brought back so many memories for me. You need to take that on the road." I said, "Oh Sam, it's so much work." But he continued, "That's why it's great, and I want you to promise me the next time I see you, you'll be with the Hee Haw people, wearing your little red dress." That was the last time I was with Sam. He passed away a year and a half later.

After Sam's death, they held a memorial for him at the Nashville Palace. Our former Hee Haw production assistant Marcia Minor and Danny Forbes organized it, and almost all of the remaining Hee Haw cast attended. Most were dressed in black...except Misty Rowe. I was wearing my bright red Hee Haw dress. I'm sure a few people thought, "Why would she wear that to a memorial?" They found out the reason, when I got up to speak. I told how Sam had instructed that the next time he saw me, he wanted me in that dress, and he wanted me with the Hee Haw people."

As I continued my tribute, I said, "I have known two great Italians in my life. One was Arthur Fonzarelli and the other was Sam Lovullo. While one was the fictional character of 'The Fonz' on 'Happy Days,' the other was a real man, who was such a strong force, who had done so much for me and my family."

After I spoke, I visited with Roy Clark. It would be the last time I would see him. I miss that lovely man so much. As the memorial went on, Ronnie Stoneman performed, and Jana Jae got out the blue fiddle she had played on Hee Haw, and I danced as she played. Everyone loved it so much, that Jana was inspired to put on a touring show called Kornfield Friends. It included Jana, Buck Trent, Lulu Roman, and me. We used the huge cornfield that Faye Sloan created for my original Hee Haw Honeys show. I still have the cornfield out in my shed. You just never know when that corn will pop out again for a new production of some kind.

HAPPY DAYS ARE HERE AGAIN

When I was working with Donny Most on "Happy Days" back in the mid-70s, I never dreamed I would be working with him again 45 years later. Of course, Don was known for his Ralph Malph character on "Happy Days," but he is also a wonderful singer. He has a great voice for swing and big band music.

After I left the "Happy Days," show we never saw each other again. But a couple years ago, we reconnected through Facebook. Donny had seen a story that Fox News had done on me, and he sent me a Facebook message. He told me he was going to be performing his big band music at a concert in North Carolina, and he asked me to come see him. It was a four and a half hour drive, but I told him I wouldn't miss it.

Then, Donny called and said, "Since you are coming to the show, why don't we sing a duet?" I explained, "Donny, I don't sing big band. I'm a country girl, and I mainly do funny songs."

He said, "Let's do 'Makin' Whoopee.' I'll send you the track so you can practice it." I'm so glad I practiced, because when we arrived at the theater, I found out Donny had been advertising me as his special guest, and the show was totally sold out.

Halfway through his show, when Donny introduced me, I was shocked at the huge ovation I received. And I was even more surprised at the applause that came after we sang our duet. Donny instantly started thinking about how he could make me a part of his act.

A short time later, we had put together a full show, that featured Donny singing songs like "Mack the Knife" and me singing Marilyn Monroe's "Diamonds Are a Girl's Best Friend." Thank you Mel Tormé for those singing lessons so many years ago! I wore my hot pink, Marilyn evening gown, and I think that dress got a bigger applause than my singing. While my gown is glamorous, given my "Hee Haw" history, I am also the show's comic attraction. Donny was the comedian on "Happy Days," but he is very comfortable giving me most of the laugh lines during our show.

In January of 2020, we performed at a talent buyer's showcase in New York. Thousands of theaters and concert venues use that event to book their entertainment for the next year. When our showcase was over, people were hugging and kissing us and taking pictures. The buyers were booking us left and right, and we knew we had something very special.

Then the Covid 19 hit, and everything came to a complete stop. Every concert and show around the country for 2020 was cancelled. But the great blessing for us was, all the bookings from the talent showcase were for 2021! So, there is a good chance that Donny and I will be coming to a town near you sometime in the near future, and we hope you'll come out and see us in person!

My fan club president, Sandi Bria is also a huge "Happy Days" fan. When I told her I was going to be performing with Donny, she flew in from Connecticut to see the concert. Donny and his wife Morgan invited us all to dinner, and we had a wonderful time. Sandi was so excited to be there, and I thought this would be a good place to ask her to share a few of her memories from our time together:

"I loved the show Happy Days, but my husband's favorite show was Hee Haw. His favorite part of the show was with Misty and Junior Samples and their BR-549 car lot. My husband always teased me, saying, 'You see that hot blonde with the high voice? That's why I watch it.' When Misty came on, he'd say, 'There's my girlfriend.'

A short time after my husband passed away, I was lonely, and I started going to a local line-dancing club. I went there quite a few times, and one night, I was totally shocked when I saw Misty walk in. I watched her, and she was too shy to even get out on the dance floor.

I walked up and introduced myself and was just in awe of her. I couldn't believe this 'movie star,' a person who was in my favorite show was here in our small town. But Misty didn't act like a star; she acted like a woman who needed a friend.

I kept her company the rest of the evening, and we became instant friends.

Misty was in the process of writing a number of plays and stage productions. When she told me she wasn't a very good typist, I volunteered to type everything for her. When I got to her house, I saw huge piles of unopened mail. I asked what it was, and she said, 'Oh, that's fan mail. But I don't have time to read it all.'

She was getting over 20 letters and autograph requests a day, and they were piling up quickly. I was surprised that some were from as far away as Switzerland and Denmark. I told her, 'I can't believe people in Switzerland watch Hee Haw!' I told her I would open it all and help her respond, and that turned into me becoming her Fan Club president.

When we first met, I was struggling financially, after the death of my husband. Misty was also struggling to pay her bills after her divorce. One day, she gave me an envelope filled with money. She said, 'I keep this envelope for women who need a little help. You can use how much you need. If you can ever pay me back, just put it in the envelope and give it back.' I had only known her for a short time, and I couldn't believe her generosity. I repaid all the money two months later and gave her the envelope back, but I never forgot what she did for me. Who knows how many women she has given that envelope to.

I went on to run a pre-school and I watched over Misty's daughter Dreama there.

I was at my day-care when I received a phone call I will never forget. I had wanted to do something special for Misty's 50th birthday, so I borrowed her address/phone book and contacted every celebrity she had listed. I asked each one to write something to her for a birthday book I was making for her.

I had a baby in my arms when the day-care phone rang. My son answered it and said, 'Mom, you have a call from a "Hef" from California.' It was Hugh Hefner, calling to confirm my request. I talked to him, as I continued holding a crying baby. I thought, 'This has to be the first daycare center that Hugh Hefner has ever called.'

With Misty Rowe, just going someplace like Home Depot is an adventure. I never liked going there, because I could never find what I was looking for, and I could never get anyone to assist me. But when I went to Home Depot with Misty, every employee came running out to help her. I stood there by myself, while there were 15 guys around her. It was ridiculous!

When I was at my lowest point in life, I think God brought Misty into my life. I love her dearly.

She is very caring and just a wonderful person. She is also very creative and very talented. She gave me a new purpose and brought so much fun and excitement to my life. My only regret is that my husband didn't live long enough to meet Misty. He would have loved her so much more than he did when he was watching her on TV. The first time Misty came to visit me in my home, I looked up to Heaven and said, 'Well, your girlfriend is here.' He wouldn't have believed that the hot blonde was now my best friend."

- Sandra Bria

STILL A HEE HAW HONEY

When I started on Hee Haw, I was 21 years old. At the time, Grandpa Jones was unbelievably, only 59, and Minnie Pearl was 60 years old. Now, even more unbelievable, I am 70 years old. I am a decade older than Grandpa Jones and Minnie Pearl were when I first met them!

Today, I am thankful to still be in good health. I have some pain in my knees, due to arthritis, but I still tap dance in the kitchen almost every day.

I've tried to always take good care of myself. I've never sunbathed or tanned. I credit that to a comment I received from actress Polly Bergen. I was on a beach in Acapulco when I was 21 years old, and I ran into Polly Bergen and her husband Freddie Fields. Freddie asked Polly to advise me against staying out of the sun, but instead, Polly looked at me and said, 'Why should I? There's nothing more I would like than when she's 25, that her skin looks like she's 40 years old.'

From that moment on, I stayed out of the sun. When I take walks on the beach, after putting on lots of sunscreen, I wear a big hat and sunglasses. My husband also brings along a beach umbrella! I almost never leave the house without sunglasses, not because I am trying to be a "star," but I wear them to protect my eyes, even on cloudy days.

We live on an island off South Carolina, and it is the perfect place to age gracefully. Many days, I don't put on any makeup. I'm very blessed to have a husband who thinks I'm beautiful without makeup. Of course, he is getting older and doesn't see very well!

Even when I'm all covered up, and even in our quite remote home, people still recognize me, and I'm grateful for that. The first thing they usually recognize is my voice. As I'm checking out or buying groceries, the person behind the counter, or behind me in line, will ask, "Were you on Hee Haw?' When I walk around our island, I'll pass people, and then I hear them whisper, "There's the Hee Haw lady."

We all grow older (if we're lucky), and I don't want to worry about my looks. I just want to be me. As you mature, you find you are not as vain as you used to be. No, I don't have the same waist I did when I was 21, but I'm OK with that, and so are most of my fans. They still turn out to see me perform, and I am thankful for each and every one of them.

I'm actually getting to know many of my fans on a much more personal level these days. Thanks to the internet and Facebook, I'm able to connect with fans and friends from around the world. I always have more than 1, 000 people waiting for me to OK them to be my Facebook "friend", but I only add a few each day. I make sure they're real and I actually try to say a few words to each person. I try to answer everyone's questions and respond to their posts. Sometimes it can get a little overwhelming, but I enjoy it.

You can find almost anything on the internet. I even found out I was married to someone I had never heard of! My Wikipedia page states that I had been married three times. I have not, and I have never met the man they list as my second husband. I also found a website someone had created to celebrate "Misty Rowe's Feet!" Now, that is crazy.

Another crazy thing happened in 2004. Michael Sansonia, the musical director for "A Misty Christmas," asked me, "Do you know there is a song about you?" It was by a rock band out of Austin, Texas, called "Young Heart Attack," and the song was titled, simply, "Misty Rowe."

I didn't believe him, and it is such a hard rock song, that it took me a long time to understand any of the lyrics, but Michael played it for me, and it talks about me as Wendy the Car Hop on "Happy Days," me as Marilyn Monroe, and they sing my name throughout the song.

When my daughter heard it, she could make out all the words easier than I could, and she was not pleased, because some of them said that I took drugs. Dreama got in touch with the leader of the band, and he explained that the song was a tribute to me. Dreama told them they should try to change their lyrics a little, since I had never done drugs in my life.

But I really took the song as a great compliment. I was happy that I made such an impression on them when they were kids and teenagers, that they would want to write a song about me. I figure that is a much better tribute than a website about my feet!

While I was writing this book, Kenny Rogers died. And a few months later, actress/sportscaster and former Miss America, Phyllis George passed away. I was blessed to know both Kenny and Phyllis through my dear friend Marianne Gordon. I've talked about Kenny earlier in this book. But Phyllis' death hit me especially hard, since she was the same age as I.

Phyllis and I were so different. The same year I was on the Overdrive Truckers magazine cover, Phyllis was crowned Miss America. She was much more high class than I was, but she was always so gracious and loving to me. She had such a great spirit and was always an inspiration.

When Phyllis died, mortality hit me right in the face. I thought, "Misty, you better start writing faster to make sure you get that book done." Of course, so many of the TV and movie stars I've worked with are now gone. The majority of our Hee Haw family are now in the big Kornfield in the sky.

I appear at quite a few celebrity memorabilia and autograph shows around the country. As you get older, your line gets longer and you think, "Wow, I must be getting popular again." But many are in your line because they know your autograph will be worth more after you die! You know the ones who will be trying to sell them. If you ask, "Would you like me to inscribe this to you?" they'll say, "No, don't personalize it to anyone. Just sign your name." Yeah, I know that will be for sale on eBay. But that's OK, I don't mind. I'll just try to outlive them, and that will show them!

I do not have any plans to retire. I figure if Betty White can work up until she's almost 100, I can perform in some way for another three decades. I can see myself on stage, on TV or directing or producing something for many years to come. I have written a play called "Forget Me Not" based on my mother's battle with Alzheimer's. I would like to see that produced. While none of us knows what the future holds, I hope that mine will include me singing, acting, telling jokes, writing, and directing for as long as possible.

Doing this book has been such a wonderful experience for me. When I started, I was very anxious. But as I looked through all my memorabilia, photos and yellowed press clippings, as I really went back through my entire life, I dredged up memories I had long forgotten. It turned out to be like a very long therapy session.

Writing your autobiography gives you the feeling of seeing your life flash before your eyes. For me, it also served as a reminder of all the people who helped me throughout my life. From my mom, making stage curtains out of bed sheets, so I could perform in our garage, to my drama teacher Mrs. Reiner, to Willie Billmeyer, who gave clothes, and so much hope to a little girl; to Stella Adler and Estelle Harmon for all the support and guidance they gave me, and to Minnie Pearl's words of wisdom on how to treat my fans. Without those women and many other women and men, I would never have achieved the success I did.

As we come to the end of this chapter (of the book and of my life), I'm sad that it's over. But I know a new chapter is about to begin, and I will be excited to see how that one turns out.

Quite a few years ago, I wrote a poem that summed up my Hee Haw career and my life. I guess this would be a good place to share it:

THE OTHER SIDE OF THE KORNFIELD

It was the man who played the banjo, and a lady with a price tag on her hat.

Pretty girls in low-cut dresses, a Kornfield and a haystack.

A squeaky voiced blonde could be a comic and even fix a car,

While Buck Owens led the mayhem, with a red, white and blue guitar.

Oh, I did so many other things, why, I even played Monroe.

But that stubborn little donkey would never really let me go.

Now that it's all behind, at last I clearly see,

That the years I spent on Hee Haw were as sweet as they could be.

For the times that I remember are just the same as you.

And sharing these memories have made new dreams come true.

PARTING SONG

I loved Misty Rowe when I was a teenager. I love her much more today.

Two years ago, I helped Lulu Roman write her autobiography. As Misty read that book, she found out what a big fan I was of hers. In the book, Lulu mentioned that I was such a big fan that I had bought Misty's bed.

It was the bed she used in her "Misty's Bedtime Stories" sketches on Hee Haw. Country Music memorabilia collector Robbie Wittkowski had owned the bed for many years. A few years ago, Robbie sold the bed to me. He laughed as I told him, "Now, I've got to come up with a story to explain this purchase to my wife."

Robbie passed away as we were writing this book. I had been looking forward to giving him a copy. I know it would have made his day.

Misty enjoyed Lulu's book (and the bed story) so much, that she decided to contact Lulu's assistant Kim Tygart to ask for my number. I was thrilled just to get a message from Misty, and when she called later, I tried to "play it cool", as so many memories of all of her TV and movie appearances came flooding back to me. I never missed an episode of Hee Haw or Happy Days, and I had watched every other TV show and movie Misty had been in.

At the time of her initial call, I reluctantly told her I was too busy to help write her book. I was working on four others, and the fact that we lived so far away from each other was also another huge obstacle. But we agreed to stay in touch.

A few months, and a few calls later, Misty's husband asked if I might be interested in working with her, through the new internet video technology called Zoom. I really didn't think it would work, but I agreed to give it a try. Over the next six months, Misty and I wrote this entire book via Zoom. We were never together in person.

As you've just read, Misty Rowe has lived a very colorful, exciting and eventful life. She has been rich and poor. She's loved and lost and loved again. She's had ups and downs, with amazing achievements and horrible heartache. After all of that, Misty still has an innocence and child-like quality about her. That quality is something you don't see in many 70-year-olds.

Thank you for letting me help you tell your story, Misty. What a wonderful person you are.

Scot England